100 Days

TO A MORE AWARE YOU

To my son, Mika,

I wish you to always remember who you truly are – a powerful creator, who gets to choose how to experience life.

Thank you for being my greatest teacher!

I love you beyond what any words could ever convey.

INTRODUCTION

This book came to life not from me, but through me. This is *her* story.

It all started with an idea that took off like a storm and quickly gained momentum. It was a quiet night at the end of September. Everyone was in bed, and I was relaxing on the terrace, looking at the stars and letting my mind wander aimlessly. Suddenly, a thought crossed my mind. There were approximately one hundred days left till the end of the year. What if, I thought, I serve my community by committing to writing and publishing on Instagram one hundred posts, one post a day, for each day until the end of the year. What if I shared all the lessons, reflections, and questions, as well as the beliefs that I hold (and the beliefs that I dropped), that have helped me set the foundation for a much more joyful, peaceful, and awakened life?

Throughout the month of September, prior to this quiet evening under the stars, I hosted free twenty-minute private calls with followers from Instagram each Wednesday afternoon. People booked the calls because they believed I could help. They had questions in various areas, with topics that varied based on their own circumstances and needs. But there was a common thread. They felt, based on my work, or based on my stories and posts, that I might have the answers they were looking for.

Upon reflection, although the idea of writing "100 Days to a More Aware You" didn't stem directly from these calls and interactions, I feel that they might have acted as a creative catalyst for the realisation. The realisation that this was one clear way for me to serve more. All I wanted was to share something that has worked well for me, something that has served me greatly in my own personal quest for inner peace, something that came from my heart. If something has served me (and others) so well, and if people wanted to know what it was, then I believe it is a calling to share it all.

And there I was, one hundred days before the end of the year, announcing the "100 Days to a More Aware You" series.

All one hundred posts reflect the following: I shared my truth, the way I felt it, and I was living it. I shared it plainly, as it was, without preaching or being pretentious.

All one hundred posts were written day after day, never prepared in advance, never bulked up, and never "researched" or planned. I wrote the post on the day I published it. Some days the writing was flowing. Some days it wasn't. There were also days when I felt I didn't have anything to share. A thought would briefly cross my mind - maybe I should look for inspiration, or research and write on a popular topic. I'm glad I didn't. I might have spent hours staring at the empty file in front of me until the message came, yet, I chose to reach out to my deep trust instead. Trust that what is meant to come out as a message for the day, will inevitably show up, every day, with no exception.

And it did! When I took the time to pause, wait patiently and turn inwards instead. I knew right from the start, that I didn't want to write for the sake of writing, or from my head, and I definitely did not want to write something that I hadn't experienced or applied in my life myself.

This book contains my personal reflections, insights, observations and beliefs. They have been, of course, largely inspired by many teachers before me (Eckhart Tolle, Michael Singer, Don Miguel Ruiz, the teachings of Abraham Hicks, to name a few). But they were, and are, all applied, felt, realised, experienced and lived by me, at that moment in time. These reflections became poetry to me. They appear here before you as they did in my journal, flaws and all. As true and raw now, as they were then. It's not a destination we get to arrive at. It's a journey.

I aimed to match each post with an image from my personal photo library that illustrates and supports the message of the post. Some did great, some didn't. Sometimes I couldn't find a photo that corresponded as well as I felt it could, but I did my best. It was a "figuring-it-out-as-you-go" process, each day, for one hundred days. I would love it if these images fulfilled the aim of illuminating and supporting the messages and that they provide you, the reader, with a beautiful book that acts as a guide. A guide that supports you in your journey of bringing more awareness, so that you can live fully in service of your own calling and reconnect with your inner powerful wisdom.

The key to happiness and personal freedom is awareness.
My wish is that this book serves you greatly in your own path to self-awareness.

I wish you a happy and fulfilling journey.

Love,
Didi

Life is magical and beautiful and messy…
And we mostly go through it asleep.

What if…

We take five minutes a day to reconnect with our inner wisdom,
bring awareness and presence to our day,
and deepen our connection within?

What if...

You spend five minutes a day...
for the next 100 days...

BECOMING A MORE AWARE YOU

Does this bring me joy?

The question that changed my life. Simple, yet powerful, and a question that we hardly ever get to ask ourselves.

Here we are…living life…getting jobs, picking projects, meeting people, making friends, raising babies, finding partners, buying stuff, changing jobs, looking for a purpose, maintaining hobbies…we are doing it all.

And we forget to ask the most important question.

Does *this* bring me joy?

This job that I was looking for, the project I said "Yes" to, the friends I surrounded myself with, the quotidian I create for myself, the way I parent, the people I meet, the conversations I engage in, the house I live in, the thoughts I think, the words I use… the way I get to live my life…

Does this bring *me* joy?

To me. Not to my mom. Not to my parents. Not to my friends, not to my colleagues, not to my partner. To *me*. Does this bring *me* joy?

We often say *yes* to things because we feel it is the right thing to do. We feel compelled, obliged, we feel it is expected of us (or we put the expectations on ourselves for the wrong reasons).

We say *yes* when we would rather say *no*. We say *yes*, even if it will suck the joy out of us. We are not even aware of why we do what we do.

Does *this* bring ME joy?

Ask this question for everything and anything you do, want, say, think, or create. Ask every day, multiple times a day.

I promise you, you will be surprised by the answers you will get from within. You will probably find it difficult to answer in the beginning. Keep asking.

Does this bring me joy?
Listen for the answer.

And then, it is up to you to decide if you are still doing it, having it, thinking it, living it, being it.

But at least now you are AWARE.

Does *this* bring me joy?

It's no wonder that Marie Kondo (@mariekondo) created a whole movement and a successful business based on this one single question.

Does *this* bring me joy!?
If not - discard it.
Or fall in love with it.

WHAT BRINGS ME JOY?

Ask a child and they will answer in a split second. The ice-cream, the hug, the dog, playing with a friend.

Ask an adult and watch them pause… searching for an answer…

It should be easy, right?

After all, we all came here to experience joyful living, and it should be pretty easy to know what brings us JOY.

And yet, sometimes during late childhood… entering adolescence, we got more are more disconnected from joy. So much that most of us don't even know *what* brings us joy…

Now do this:
Take a pen and paper. Set an alarm for five minutes. Start writing as fast as you can, without overthinking it…everything that comes to mind that brings YOU joy.

Everything that comes to mind, without censoring it!

Write it down, even if a part of you is already quickly judging you… for that small/big/weird/crazy/irrelevant thing that you put on the list.

Stop writing. Look at your list but be aware of your own judgement. Thank yourself for the time you spent writing this list. Set the intention to experience more of the joys you just put on the list. Now that it is there, in 'physical' form, trust that you will find the time to experience more of it in your life.

Look at your list often. Do more of what's on it. Feel the joy!

And if you find this exercise really difficult at this moment, this is okay! You're not alone. Thank yourself for giving it a go and go back to asking yourself throughout the day, multiple times a day, when you engage in any activity or thought process 'Does THIS bring ME joy?'. This will very soon bring you awareness about what brings you joy and what doesn't.

HEAR YOUR THOUGHTS...
AND DON'T BELIEVE THEM

The mind creates its own thoughts, usually automatically. Based on past experiences, beliefs and programming. Thoughts are running in your mind constantly… this voice in your head…the Judge.

Hear your thoughts… and don't believe them.

Almost all of what you hear isn't true.
Be skeptical of what you hear, be in doubt.

Hear your thoughts, and let go of the desire to control them (this is hardly possible). Hear your thoughts…and don't believe anything you hear.

Thoughts create emotions, emotions are vibrations. You can't control the thought (that takes too much effort), but what you can do is - let it go. Most of the thoughts running in our head are negative. Thoughts of constant judgement, fear, scarcity. Let them go. They aren't true.

Be aware of their pattern.

Take five minutes today to listen to your thoughts without judgement or reaction. Sit down, close your eyes, and let your mind run freely, without intention or expectation. Hear your thoughts… and don't believe them. Let them go.

Now you are aware.

———

I highly recommend to read *Untethered Soul* by Michael Singer and *The Fifth Agreement* by Don Miguel Ruiz

DON'T BE IN A HURRY...

Don't be in a hurry to act, to judge, to say what you thought you meant. Don't be in a hurry to get it all done, to bring it on, to start it, to finish it…

Yes, our society still rewards and promotes being in a hurry. We live in a state of constant rush and we put ourselves under unnecessary stress. We seldom pause to reflect.

But you can decide.

You can still choose to be in a hurry. And if you do, let it be for a kind gesture, for a smile to a stranger, for making someone feel good, seen and special today. Let it be for bringing out this feeling of appreciation that is always in you, but it is often buried under layers of worry, guilt, anxiety, and to-do lists.

Take five minutes today and ask yourself these questions:

Where am I in a hurry right now? What am I rushing? What's behind it?

Bring awareness to it.

Then you can decide if it is worth it.

HOW RELAXED CAN YOU BE?

Years ago, before I got pregnant and during pregnancy, I used to regularly attend a hatha yoga class at my local gym. My teacher's name was Nicola. I still hear her voice in my head, almost ten years later.

"How relaxed can you be?" she'd say.

She would put us in these challenging poses that we had to hold, sometimes for a long time, and she would say in her sweet, quiet voice: "Now, how relaxed can you be?"

To date, this is my mantra. When I'm doing something uncomfortable, or I'm attempting a new exercise regime, or I'm shipping my work, or I'm preparing for a meeting, I stop and ask myself:

"How relaxed can you be?"

Right now, at this moment.

It has always shifted my awareness from the problem, the challenge, the issue to the present moment, helping me realise that I *can* relax, right now, in the midst of it.

"How relaxed can you be?"

Give it a go right now. Close your eyes, get quiet and ask yourself: "How relaxed can you be?"

Focus on the question, mindfully become the observer of your body and mind.

And next time when you feel rushed, challenged or overwhelmed, ask again:

How relaxed can YOU be?

I still ask myself this question with Nicola's voice, using *you* instead of *I*. If we are to have another inner voice (and we all do, multiple ones, often unaware of it), let it be one that brings you light and joy.

WHAT IF IT ISN'T TRUE?

The thought that runs through your mind, this statement you heard and agreed with, the phrase that you just uttered, the "facts" that you know "for sure"…

What if it isn't *true*?

We shape our reality through the beliefs we hold. And we have accumulated and internalised beliefs that we have never examined, and rarely even noticed. From early childhood, we were exposed to the beliefs of our families, society, teachers, preachers, peers, and trusted adults. Soon, we started to believe what they believed. No bad intentions, on the contrary - this is truly what they believed too, and it was only natural to pass it on.

Very few of these beliefs are true. And even fewer serve us well.

Examine your beliefs. Start by asking:

"What if this isn't true?" Ask often, on repeat, about everything that crosses your mind, fuels your actions, or comes up in a conversation.

Be doubtful of everything!

It doesn't have to be hard, you don't have to "effort" through it. It doesn't even have to take a long time.

The more you ask, the more aware you'll become of the beliefs you hold.

What if this isn't true?

Ask often, on repeat, about everything….

Make it a daily practice.

And if a belief doesn't serve you well - let it go…

Take your power back.

WHAT DO I RESIST RIGHT NOW? WHAT DO I PUSH AGAINST?

Resistance keeps your attention on the unwanted things.

And the harder you try, the more you practice resistance.

(Yes, we were all taught the virtue of trying harder. But what if this isn't true?)

Pushing against something is detrimental and keeps you focused on the exact thing you don't want.

What if...

What if you practice the path of least resistance?

Nature flows with it beautifully.

Take five minutes right now. Sit down and close your eyes. Take seven slow breaths. Get quiet, stay still, and ask: What do I resist right now? Listen carefully.

Acknowledge your resistance. It is the first step to breaking free from it.

In the wise words of author Eckhart Tolle:

"To offer no resistance means to be in a state of grace, ease and lightness."

"Resist nothing."

THERE IS ONLY ONE OF YOU

You are unique and you never existed before as *you*. Consciousness expressed itself through you, in you, in this time and space reality.

You, right now in this physical body…you and your mind, soul and heart…are unique and unrepeated.

There is only one of you.

You are the artist, the powerful creator and *you* get to choose what to put on your canvas.

People may say they know better than you do. Even you may assume that they know better than you do.

People may teach you, guide you, coach you, educate you. That's great.

But remember…there is only one of *you* and no one truly knows *you*.

We often forget this. We look for the answers outside of us. We copy others, we look for recipes from others. We delegate our happiness, joy and creativity to others. We assumed that they must know better. And they might do, but only in regards to them. Not to you. As there is only one of you…

Do not outsource your life's work.

It might be uncomfortable to disappoint others or to assume responsibility. But you are here to expand and grow and enjoy this time and space reality…as *you*.

And there is only one of you…

CAN YOU SEE THE WORLD THROUGH THE EYES OF A CHILD?

Can you see the world through the eyes of a child?
With the freshness of their innocence...

Without labels and concepts, without preconceived ideas and judgements.

Seeing the beauty of the world as it is, pure and wonderful, joyful and magical.

Through the eyes of the child, we will be curious, eager and ready to explore, excited to learn, to grow, to absorb everything that there is...

- Time won't matter.
- Things or people won't be either good or bad.
- There will be no competition.
- Differences will be curiously observed and accepted, rather than judged.
- Interests will be followed.
- Emotions will be allowed and accepted.
- Past will be left alone.
- Future won't be constantly considered.
- Present will be all that there is.

When we see through the eyes of a child, we will live our lives in wonder.

Can you see the world through the eyes of a child?
Not all the time, but maybe most of the time... or at least sometimes.

A BEGINNER...

The older we get and the more expertise we gain in an area, the harder it gets for us to be *beginners*. Early in life, we don't mind it. We might even enjoy it. But soon, after we graduate from school and take on a path of study or work, we build expertise in certain areas and we start avoiding the beginner stage.

We enjoy being knowledgeable, being the experts. We enjoy knowing the answers. And it's natural. We come to this life with an inherent need to contribute and give, and sharing our knowledge is part of that.

But, also, the Ego loves it! We attach value to our knowledge, and it provides us with a sense of power and worthiness.

And this can be a slippery slope. We start to avoid trying new things. We feel uncomfortable when we are unknowledgeable. We keep doing what we have been doing. Sometimes our expertise, if unexamined, can hinder our growth.

Recently, I was exercising alongside my sister. We got to the squats part of the video, and I was about to tell my sister how to do the squat. I stopped myself, as I realised she had more experience than me.

This made me think, though, how flawed and even harmful the "expert mindset" can be.

We can be experts in a certain area, bringing years of experience, but it can lead to doing things automatically, seeing situations in a certain way, or being biased based on the expertise we hold. We can become more reluctant to try new things or new strategies, or new ways of doing things. When we approach the mindset of a newbie, we can provide freshness and innovation.

I remembered launching my school years ago. How uncomfortable it was at times… my feeling deep inside that I was new to this industry and my team was more experienced. I also remembered how my fresh look led to many beautiful initiatives and shook the status quo that has not been necessarily explored.

What if we adopted the beginner's mindset for everything we do?

Words are powerful and the word "beginner" carries (for many) a negative connotation. Compare it to the word "advanced" or "accelerated".

Sit with the word and unwrap its meaning… to you. Once aware, you can redefine this meaning.

Where in life can you adopt the beginner's mindset right now?

WHAT'S NORMAL FOR YOU?

Normal means conforming to a standard; usual, typical, or expected.

What's normal for me, might be unusual to you and vice versa.

We live our life defined by our "normal", and our behaviour (and mindset) is shaped by what's "normal" to us.

This is great news! Because if you want to change something in your life, you can "normalise" it.

How?

By creating a favourable environment for it to become "normal". By surrounding yourself with people for whom the things you want to be, have or do are pretty normal. By diving into information that supports this "normal".

Soon it will become your new "normal" too, and your reality will reflect this.

A few years ago, I asked a very successful friend of mine, who runs three large businesses in three different industries across continents while travelling, "How do you manage to run these complex businesses while travelling so frequently?", because for me each travel was taking me out of the workflow and his travel was a long haul.

His answer: "Well, I don't know any different. My parents have always been doing the same things. I grew up like this, I guess I never thought I might not be able to do it."

Bang! This was very NORMAL to him.

It made me so aware of my *normal*. And I am fully aware that it is up to me to create a new normal in any area of my life.

How aware are you of your normal? What is something in your life right now that you would love to "normalise"? Write that down, explore it, and change it if you wish.

HOW GOOD CAN YOU ALLOW?

I borrowed this from my friend Yanik (@yaniksilver) who shared how this question came up during his meditation.

"How good can you allow?"

What is it in us, adults, that prevents us from absorbing every ounce of goodness and joy without guilt, without the almost immediate judgement that we impose on ourselves promptly, and without the overwhelming fear that we might soon lose what we now feel?

Depending on your culture and upbringing, you may carry strong beliefs about how much good is good for you. I certainly did, hearing it repeated far too many times by the adults in my culture:

- Too much good is not good…
- Don't say you are feeling good, because you're asking for trouble.
- Don't relax into feeling good, as it won't last long and you will attract something bad.
- Don't even say you feel good, because people will be jealous and you will attract bad energy.

I can keep going…

As if the Universe, like a masterful accountant, keeps a balance sheet in which all good things must be balanced by equally bad.

It took me time and awareness to get rid of these beliefs, which still crawl back if I slip into unconsciousness. It took me awareness to realise that there was no balance sheet and there was no offsetting.

It is the opposite.

Good feeling thoughts attract more good feeling thoughts. The better it gets, the better it gets. The vibration of positive emotions and joy is higher and it is easier to keep it high by doing, feeling and experiencing more of the good things.

This is how the Law of Attraction works.

This is also why when we are in love, everything seems to be working out so well in all areas of our lives.

We hardly ever fully and deeply relax, even when we feel connected and aligned. We fear it will be over. And we rather get it over ourselves... right now.

Observe a little child fully immersed in their joyful activity...without guilt or fear. Watch how much good they allow naturally, as it was meant to be, without any guilt or fear. When and how did we lose that?

How good can you allow?

Sit with this question today.

Bring awareness to it.

Allow the good…

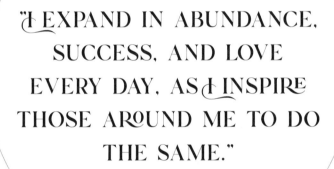

"I EXPAND IN ABUNDANCE, SUCCESS, AND LOVE EVERY DAY, AS I INSPIRE THOSE AROUND ME TO DO THE SAME."

Gay Hendricks

CAN YOU SEE IT BETTER THAN IT IS?

Some time ago, I heard Tony Robbins speaking about leadership. He said that two of the many qualities of great leaders were that they:

1) See things as they are (not worse than they are), and that they:
2) See them better than they are.

Our view of the world will always be subjective and flawed. We shape our reality through our perception and focus. In time, how we perceive things becomes habitual, defined by our identity, beliefs, habits, and patterns.

It is up to us to CHOOSE how we see the world. It is also up to us to change our point of attraction.

We can tell better-feeling stories about our lives and life situations. We can consciously choose to focus on what we want to be, have or do instead of perceiving our circumstances as they are right now (and how they are right now is mostly how they were yesterday).

Of course, we can also do the opposite - see it as worse than it is. This is far easier and quite prevalent. Complaining and whining serve us a purpose, and the Ego thrives on it. It is easy to dive into negativity and complaints, and it is even easier to get stuck in its energy.

It's *your* choice.

Can you see it *better* than it is?

It's well worth the initial effort. Soon enough, the momentum will put things into motion, supporting you in changing your point of attraction. Your reality will "catch up" with how you see your world.

It is up to you.

———

I recommend reading *A Complaint Free World* by Will Bowen and *Vortex* by Esther Hicks. I find them helpful to adapt this mindset.

Day 14

CAN YOU LOVE YOURSELF AS DEEPLY AS YOU LOVE YOUR CHILD?

Can you love yourself as deeply as you love your child? With an unconditional, intense, unshakeable love, not based on judgements or prejudice... the way you love a baby, purely and deeply, acknowledging their beauty - a perfect expression of life?

Can you love yourself the way you love a child?

Or even better, can you love yourself the way your young child loves *you*?

No flaws, no judgement, no desire or a need to change you. You are accepted and loved, just the way you are.

Our usual state is one where we feel inadequate, unseen, judged, or criticised. And no matter how strong the outer criticism is, the one that hurts us the most is the inner one, our own. We feel that we are not enough and we feel we are not worthy of love.

What if...

What if, today...right now... you pause, and remember:

How easy is it to love your child... a child...the way they are?

And there is nothing that is expected from them,

as they are perfect the way they are.

And so *you* are too.

31

WHAT'S YOUR "HARD"?

We saw the group of children, and we stopped to watch the fun. My seven-year-old son, Mika, and I were passing by the group a few months ago in Hyde Park. The kids, fifteen of them, between the ages of five and nine, were attending a multi-skills gym class. The coach was giving them instructions on their run challenges. They were all running at a given signal to the little poles a few metres away and back, competing in teams to be the first. The coach was cheering and everyone was excited about their team. When they finished one of their runs, the coach gave them his next instructions.

He said: "Team, listen carefully. Tell me, how can we make this run harder? Any suggestions?"

The kids, including Mika and myself, started eagerly sharing their suggestions: "We can run with our eyes closed; we can walk backwards; we can wheel cart each other, we can grass walk like snakes, etc."

They were full of ideas and they were all having FUN, exploring the harder solutions.

I was fascinated! It suddenly struck me how much heaviness we put on the word "hard".

Hard can be FUN. Hard can be welcomed. Yes, by definition, hard means "done with a great deal of effort", but effort is not necessarily bad. An effort is a conscious exertion of power. It doesn't necessarily mean it is a struggle.

It made me reflect while we continued on our walk….

I have been quite conscious of my use of words, especially in the past few years. I have consciously chosen to change certain beliefs, and I have explored my relationship with certain words and their meaning to me.

I have dug into the word HARD in regards to some of my beliefs, e.g. you need to work hard to be successful; hard work pays back; nothing worth it comes easy; it is hard to…(fill in the blank), change is hard, etc. I am sure you will recognise many of these yourself.

I was extra aware of where I put this word in my sentences, if at all!

And suddenly, here it was: the realisation.

I do not need to avoid the word or the activity, I can see it as FUN.

Of course, my training with my personal trainer a few months ago felt hard! And I loved it!

Of course, figuring this project out felt hard. And I loved it!

Of course, learning how to swim freestyle felt hard since I felt I was drowning. And I loved it!

Of course, studying this subject felt hard. And I loved it!

It was not about how hard something was. Not at all.

It is all about how *chosen* your "hard" feels.

When you consciously choose something to be, work on, create, activate and it comes from a place of alignment and desire, the "hard" element feels fun! It brings joy and it inspires you to keep going. You enjoy the "hardness" of it.

When something feels imposed on you, outside of your control, and you have the sense that you have no choice; or when you do something that you do not enjoy, the hard is… well… really hard.

What's your "hard"? What does the word "hard" mean to you, what's your body's reaction to it?

I have done a lot of *hard* things in my life. And I have, surely, attracted many of them, through my beliefs, programming, and patterns.

Now, I am very careful about what I invite into my life. I am aware that I create and craft my life and my reality, and I choose to follow the Joy. It can come hand in hand with Hard. But it DOESN'T have to. And that's the beauty of life.

What's your "hard"?

Bring your awareness to it…

"IF YOU CHANGE THE
WAY YOU LOOK AT
THINGS, THE THINGS
YOU LOOK AT CHANGE."

Wayne Dyer

WHAT'S YOUR COMPASS?

The compass is a tool for finding direction. It makes it easier for us to find our way on the path while hiking or to determine the direction of a vessel despite the obscured sky.

Without it, we can still find our direction, but it can take us much longer and it could be unnecessarily harder.

What is your *compass*?

What helps you navigate the challenges, transitions, and changes in your life? What helps you make decisions?

When you are clear on what's important to you, and what you value, you have built a compass to help you navigate the waves of life. Each decision becomes so much easier to make, and the path ahead is clear, no matter how cloudy it is. You know where you are heading to.

What's your *compass*?

Take five minutes today. Sit down in a comfortable position. Take three deep and slow breaths, breathing fully in and out. Close your eyes and ask: "What's important to me in my life? What's important to me?" Ask it again and again…

What do I value the most?

Listen. This can be your compass. It is yours to use.

Use it to navigate your daily life. Don't lock it in a drawer…

You will be surprised at how much easier your decision-making will become. You won't need to overthink or over analyse.

You can just remember that you have a compass…

WHAT WOULD LOVE AND TRUTH DO NOW?

I learnt this from my dear friend Tracey (@tivanyshyn) who is an amazing human and an exceptional leader.

The questions…

We all go through the day with numerous decisions to make. And often, we might feel unsure, overwhelmed or even stuck, especially when the decisions involve other people (which they often do).

These questions will help you see the situation from various angles and provide perspective. They will guide you to a solution or an answer that you haven't thought of.

Ask:
What would LOVE do now?
What would TRUTH do now?

Grace, fear, courage… Replace it with any word that feels right for you in this situation.

You might be surprised by the answers that come up to you.

Day 18

THE POWER OF 10

(I wrote this post on the 10th day of the 10th month, 10/10)

Let's play.
Let's use this sacred number and bring its potency out in a joyful, fun and powerful way.

Take out your notebook. Set an alarm for 10 minutes and when ready to start, go to the questions below. You only have 10 minutes in total.

Why the short time? Because it will help you bypass the mind. Instead of overthinking your answers, you will write the first things that come to mind, often straight from your powerful intuition. Don't get stuck on a particular question, just keep going.

Write whatever comes to you without censoring it - you can reflect after you finish, but for the moment, just write it all down.

Are you ready? Pen and paper? 10-minute timer?

Let's go!

QUESTIONS
1. What are 10 things I love about myself?
2. What are 10 things I love about my kid, mom, partner, etc (choose one)?
3. What are 10 things I want to do or be by the end of the year?
4. What are 10 people in my life I love and appreciate?
5. What are 10 things I do well?
6. What are 10 things I would rather outsource/delegate?
7. What are 10 things that bring me joy?
8. What are 10 things I value?
9. What are 10 foods I love?
10. What are 10 books, movies, or songs I love?

Once you finish:
Go through your list. Where did you struggle, if you did? What do you think was the reason? What's behind the struggle? When was it easy? Why? Where did your mind try to censor you? What surprised you?

Usually, we find the questions that deal with ourselves more challenging - the things we love and appreciate in ourselves...what we are good at...what brings us joy. We might find it hard to list our wishes and desires too because the mind is speed-light fast to censor these or dismiss them as unrealistic.

Reflect upon your answer. Write down any insights. Bring awareness to the areas you'd like to explore more.

What a beautiful way to spend 10 minutes.

*Fun fact: Pythagoras thought that 10 is the most sacred number of all, because 1+2+3+4=10. The numbers represent (1) existence, (2) creation, (3) life, and (4) the elements of earth, air, fire, and water.

"AN UNAWAKENED
PERSON SEES ONLY HIS
MIND, WHICH IS MERELY
A REFLECTION OF THE
LIGHT OF PURE
CONSCIOUSNESS
ARISING FROM THE
HEART."

Ramana Maharshi

CAN YOU ASK FREELY?

Can you ask freely?

Or do you withhold your asking...feeling what you ask for is too big, too unrealistic, too materialistic or too bothersome?

Or you even feel unworthy of the ask you make...

I don't refer to asking friends or colleagues for a favour or support (although this is important too).

I am referring to asking our most wonderful ally, the powerful Universe, that is immensely cooperative and ready to deliver. I am referring to giving your desires a chance... a chance to be fulfilled, through asking freely.

Ask, and it shall be given.

If only we could ask freely! If only we wouldn't restrict and suppress our wishes....as soon as

they were conceived!

Observe carefully when an ask arises within you, no matter how big or small, what do you do? Do you let it evolve, or do you drop it on the spot? Why, when, and what's the difference?

Asking freely is a skill. As with any other skill, we get better by practising. It takes awareness to even realise what prevents us from asking freely.

I know what it was for me.
A nice cocktail of guilt, humility, and wrong beliefs.

My belief was that I shouldn't ask for small things. They don't matter in the grand scheme of things, I shouldn't bother the Universe, I will keep my asks for the big things only. As if there is a limit to the number of requests we make, and we have to keep our options for the

times we really need them. I was coming from a place of scarcity, instead of abundance.
In my definition of small things, I would allocate everything - study, work, staff, project, family, events, trips... Everything would fall into this category. The only big things in my world were health-related for my family and myself.

There were other things that prevented me from asking. I shouldn't ask for more, it is wrong to ask for stuff, what I am asking for is too out of reach, or not cool, or not sustainable, or too much, or…

Does this sound familiar?

When was the last time you let a desire fly before you grounded it?

Ask freely.

We honour the Universe with our requests. There are no big or small requests, it is all creation! And there are no limits.

Bring awareness to how you feel when you ask.
… and then work with the feeling.

Ask and feel good.

Ask and it will be given.

"THE UNIVERSE WILL
ALWAYS GIVE YOU WHAT
YOU HAVE ASKED FOR. THE
QUESTION IS: HOW SOON
WILL YOU ALLOW IT?"

Abraham-Hicks

IF IT'S HEAVY, DROP IT

If it's heavy, drop it...

Or use it to get stronger.

But don't let it exhaust you.

We sometimes carry the heavy stuff for much longer than we need to. The problem, the difficulty, the words they uttered and the traces left, the painful memory, the story…

We carry it for so long that we forget we are the ones who carry it.

You can drop it.
Right now.

And if you are not yet ready, then at least carry it intentionally and give it a purpose. In the same way you run with added weight to strengthen your muscles or carry heavy bags while hiking to the top. Use its heaviness to *grow*.

But don't let it exhaust you.

Instead, drop the weight when it has fulfilled its purpose.

HOW CAN I MAKE THIS EASIER?

I have been using this question a lot in the past year and a half. Along with my other favourite question: "Does this bring me joy?", it has contributed to a much more joyful and lighter way of living, with a focus on ease.

How can I make this easier?

In the midst of a crisis, or an overwhelm, when my mind would automatically go to a habitual stress-resolving mode, I would remember to pause and ask:

"How can I make this easier?"

It wasn't meant to be hard. The Universe doesn't mean it to be hard. It should be easy.

I remember to remember.

How can I make this *easier*?

My brain now focuses on finding the answer to this particular question, offering solutions that I would have otherwise missed. My solutions are far more creative and insightful. But most importantly, this question keeps reinforcing my newly formed belief that serves me so well: It wasn't meant to be hard.

It wasn't meant to be hard. We got it all wrong.

How can I make this easier?

Give it a go. Right now, if there is a situation, an issue, or a challenge you are dealing with. Ask a few times "How can I make this easier?" and listen for the answer. You might be surprised.

I wish you ease and flow. I hope that this question helps you as much as it has helped me.

YOU ARE DIFFERENT...

We are afraid to show we are different and we are afraid to stand out.

But we didn't come to be this way, on the contrary. We came to be with a strong sense of who we are. And soon, we forgot.

Soon, we were being programmed to be like everyone else. It is much safer to be like everyone else.

We learn this early on, at school, from family, and society. At school, we were penalised if we were different. The school taught us that the safe thing to do was to fit in.

As Seth Godin wrote: "We line kids up in straight rows, put them in batches called grades, and work very hard to make sure there are no defective parts. Nobody standing out, falling behind, running ahead... Playing it safe. Following the rules."

"The Purple cow is so rare because people are afraid." We are afraid to stand out. We are afraid to show that we are different.

And in time, we even forget that we were once different. We live in the shadow, in the safety of conformity.

Yet, we ARE different. And we have always been. There is only *one* of us.

Don't let your fear mask your brilliance.

You are different from any other human being and this is the beauty of life. Your challenge is to re-align with who you are. Who you´ve always been...

Because consciousness is expressing itself through you - the you as you came to be.

And remember, being different is not being oppositional. Being different doesn't mean pushing against anyone.

Being different means being *you*.

Synchronise with who you are and embrace it.

And you will be a great gift to many others.

IS THERE A FIGHT WORTH FIGHTING?

We fight most of the time, and often, we are not even aware of it.

We fight against other people's opinions, beliefs, and ideas.

We fight for our own opinions, beliefs, and ideas. We fight with others and we fight with ourselves.

We spent so much vital energy on *fighting*… fighting that brings more fighting…fighting that brings frustration, anger, and sadness.

And we don't realise that through *fighting*, we build a stronger field of resistance that keeps us at lower frequency levels. And that attracts more things to *fight with*.

There are many reasons why we fight:

- a cause that we believe in
- an opinion we hold
- a desire we wish to fulfil
- a habit we dislike
- a life situation we want to get out of

We can be really good at reasoning about the fight, or making sense of it…

But the truth is that fighting doesn't help us, on the contrary. It takes a lot of energy and it brings our focus on the things we don't want.

What if we drop the fight?

As soon as we become aware that we are in the midst of it…

We stop.

And focus instead on shaping the world and living our lives from a place of strong vision of the way we want it to be? Not engaging in fights with others, not engaging in fights within, but focusing instead on living from a place of being active creators?

We *create* our own reality. Would we rather fight for it, and other people's realities, or focus on building it, on strong foundations of joy, ease, and love?

Is there a fight *worth* fighting?

SET YOUR DESIRE FREE

Set your desire free.

And then follow it.

Desires are powerful. They move us towards what's calling us.

True desires make us feel alive, vibrant and connected. They support our expansion and growth.

And yet, we dismiss them.

How often we harshly judge our desires, or we lower them and discard them before we even give them a chance.

"I would love this, but…"
"I really feel I should be going for this, but…"
"I intend this, but…"

We might get excited for a while, we might even build some momentum for going after them, but it doesn't last long. Soon, we "sober" up. The "but" plays its role and highlights for us all the reasons why we shouldn't or couldn't be going after what we desire.

We let it fade away.

What if, instead, we bring our awareness to the desire,

and replace the "but" with an "and",

and keep our focus on expanding and exploring what comes after the "and"?

We will find out that soon enough, our desire will take on its own journey. Soon, it'll be flying and pulling us with it. All we have to do is to follow its lead.

When a desire is present, consciousness focuses on this exact potential. When a desire is present, we have the full capacity to achieve it. If we hadn't, we wouldn't have conceived it, it wouldn't have come to us.

You can do and be everything you desire.

Can you set your desire *free*?

And then follow it?

What if the only person evaluating me was me?

Will I change my actions, my output, my behaviour?

What will I do differently?

We all come with a need to belong, to affiliate with others, and to be socially accepted. As children, we seek our parents' approval. At school, we seek our teachers' and peers' approval. We look for their feedback, consciously or unconsciously. Soon, we are modifying our behaviour, interest, and goals, often guided by their opinion and assessment of us.

What if the only person evaluating me was me? Not my parents, not my teachers, not my boss or my colleagues.

What if I evaluated my progress, my interests, my desires based on what's important to me?

What if I align with my own truth and use it as a compass, and then take responsibility for my own progress?

Yes, I might be afraid that I'll lose friendships or lower my chances of belonging to a wider group.

Yes, I might be afraid that I'll be stuck without an external evaluation; I have counted on it so much in the past that it has now become second nature. I have already given it so much power.

I invite you to do this:

Go back in time, to your time in school. Remember your school days.

What if the only person evaluating you was you? Not your teacher and not your parents. You.

Would you have done things differently?

How?

Take some time to bring your awareness to the power you might have given away to others.

Why Do You Do What You Do?

Ask a little child and they'll tell you:

Because I want to. Because I feel like it… Because it's fun. Because it's so interesting. Because it makes me happy. Because I'm bored. Because I can.

Ask an adult, and more often they'll tell you: Because I need to. Because I have to. Because I'm responsible. Because I'm building a career. Because that's how you do it. Because that's the right thing to do. Because I don't know how else to do it.

Take five minutes today and bring awareness to your "doing". Ask yourself: Why do I do what I do?

Do you answer more like a child or more like an adult?

There are no right or wrong answers. And of course, there are many things that we DO in our daily life, and so our answers will be different. But how often is our "doing" automatic, or installed by our parents, society, or habits?

Bring awareness to your "doing" and what fuels it. Then you can decide for yourself whether it's worth it to keep doing it.

Day 27

When are you most present?

I was in a taxi from the airport to downtown. It was one of my first trips away since Mika was born. I was passing through Chicago on my way to an event. Upon arrival, I went out to explore the city that I barely knew.

I was walking outside, taking it all in, watching people, boats, buildings, embracing the buzz of the city. I stopped at the river bank and reflected: "What is it about travelling that makes us so much more present?"

For a while, the mind gets quieter.

I thought about extreme sports. What makes people choose to hang from rocks, or jump from planes? I thought about how the activity must make them fully present. It provides temporary relief from the constant mind chatter.

The mind will do everything possible to take us out of the present moment. It gets busy planning, judging, blaming, rationalising, resolving, and managing.

All spiritual teachers tell us to be present, to live in the moment, to embrace the Now. We all know it is helpful, and yet, why is it so hard to actually live in it?

We get lost in thoughts about the tasks for the day, and the plans for tomorrow, and we make long lists in our heads. We contemplate past experiences and punish ourselves for mistakes that we replay over and over again. We project in the future and we build upon the past. It is our evolutionary disposition. To the Ego, the present hardly exists.

But the present moment is all that is.

Then how do we stay in the present more effortlessly?

How do we get to practise being more in the moment?

Yes, of course, focusing on body sensations and following the breath helps. Yet, it is often not exciting or easy for many of us, so we don't do it. And if we try to force ourselves, we only build resistance.

What if instead, we focus on the question:

When am I *most* present?

I know it for myself. It is when I am in a deep conversation with another person, when I am presenting, teaching, or serving. It is when I am in nature. It is when I am laughing with my son.

When are you *most* present?

Now that you know, can you do more of it?

In time, you'll enjoy the present moment more and more, and it will be effortless to return to the Now by choice.

"LIVE THE ACTUAL
MOMENT. ONLY THIS
ACTUAL MOMENT IS LIFE."

Thích Nhất Hạnh

I WONDER...

I wonder why this is showing up right now.
I wonder what I can learn from this.
I wonder what it would look like if it were easier.
I wonder what's the gift in it.
I wonder how it would be different if I gave it all.
I wonder what if I act upon my intuition today.
I wonder how I can get more in less time.

I wonder....

Can you shift from a desire to figure it out and know the answer, to a state of wondering... much like a small child who is in constant natural wonder of the world around?

Asking an "I wonder" question is a beautiful way to access our imagination, creativity, and intuition. We operate from the mind, instantly wanting to know the answers to the questions we ask or to the ones we are asked. But what if we are okay with not knowing? What if we are curious to welcome what would show up for us when we wonder?

"I wonder" is a beautiful way to ask open-ended questions that have no right or wrong answer. "I wonder" doesn't require an answer at all. It is a question coming out of our desire to explore, out of curiosity and inquisitiveness, not out of the need to figure it all out. You may not have an answer, and that's okay. The magic is in the question.

Wonder is different from knowing. It asks you to step into the unknown, into the unfamiliar, and brings out your creative side, beyond the need to know.

I wonder what my life would look like if I lived it from a constant place of wonder.

What about you?

FIND MANY EXCUSES TO FEEL GOOD

We are really good at finding excuses to feel bad, overwhelmed, and unhappy. Of course, we would say, it is not that we want to, but the reality of life is bringing it on us. But the Ego loves drama. We glorify pain and sacrifice. We put the hardships on a pedestal and we often remind ourselves, and others, of the many difficulties we go through in our life, as if we are striving to earn a badge of honour.

And, of course, there is the guilt that many of us experience, when many good things happen to us. Why me? What about the others?

Add to it the fear. "Too good is not good, it won't last".

It is not surprising at all that life brings us many reasons not to feel good.

Do this instead.

Find many excuses to feel good every day.

Take young children, for example. They naturally gravitate toward things that make them feel good. They actively seek those things and go for them immediately.

We used to be like that too.

And then we grew up.

Can you find excuses to feel good?

WHAT DO I FORCE IN MY LIFE RIGHT NOW?

What do I force myself to do?

Who do I force myself to be?

It is wonderful to have a clear direction as to where you're going and a compass to help you get there when disoriented.

It is wonderful to know who you want to be and how you want to show up in your life for yourself and others while holding a strong vision of it.

But getting on this chosen path doesn't have to be forced. It doesn't have to be hard or difficult. It doesn't have to require a lot of effort. We often forget that the journey is far more important than the endpoint, not the other way around, as we were programmed to believe.

How often in your day do you feel like you need to force yourself to do something or to act in a certain way?

Of course, there are probably many things that we don't feel like doing. But the more we focus on the "must" in doing them, the more we push, the more we force ourselves - the more resistance we build. Then the journey is not only not enjoyable - it is overwhelming and exhausting instead.

Sit down with these questions:
What do I force myself to do right now?

If I am still choosing to do it, how can I let go of the resistance around it?

Day 31

Do Nothing

I practise this.

When I'm feeling stressed and overwhelmed when I feel triggered by events in my environment, when I'm provoked or on edge…

I do *nothing*.

I don't take any action to resolve the situation at this particular moment.

When things are not going well, when I feel that I need to be pushing and trying harder…

I pause. And I remember to do nothing.

I don't make decisions, I don't take action, I don't look for a solution.

Not from this place, not from this state.

We live in a vibrational cooperative Universe that responds to our predominant vibration.

When we are stressed, sad, tired and angry, when we are not in alignment, our vibration is low. The harder it gets, the harder it gets.

When we act from a place of anger and frustration, we are reactive to the event, instead of responding from a place of calm and harmony. A place of higher vibration.

It doesn't mean that we will not get any results from this place, but often the solution will not be as good as it would be if we waited. Often it'll be much harder to achieve what we aim for, and we pay a higher price for it all.

I remind myself that everything should be easy. The Universe never meant it to be hard. Not that it won't work out if we push hard, but it's not necessary.

If I put any effort or choose to take action, I do it towards bringing myself back to alignment. I'm reaching out towards better-feeling thoughts (in general, not in regards to the particular situation because I find it is usually harder this way); I focus on feeling good.

Often, the situation resolves on its own. Or in a few hours or days, I feel inspired to find a solution from a place of calm and clarity.

The more I practise, the better I get at it. I am more aware of the times I'm still in a reactive mode, when I still allow stress and resistance to drive my decisions. But I am getting so much better and it is so much more satisfying.

Give it a go.

Next time when you are triggered or stressed and you feel you have to find a solution and take action…

Do *nothing* instead.

Don't start with something that has higher stakes. Practice.

And see how it goes. Keep awareness of the drivers of your actions.

"THERE IS NO REASON
TO CONSTANTLY ATTEMPT
TO FIGURE EVERYTHING
OUT"

Michael A. Singer

Day 32

DOES THIS SERVE ME?

Does this serve me?

This belief…
The statement that you just shared, and I agreed with…
This memory…
The story I've been telling over and over…

Does this *serve* me?

I am the only one who can answer this question. Something that serves many others, might not be of service to me. And only I can choose whether to keep it or let it go.

Does this *serve* me?

If it does, great. Reinforce it. Live by it.
If it doesn't, great, now I know. Drop it. Let it go.

It's that simple. Once we are aware, it is really

that simple.

The difficulty comes when we are not aware that we hold unhelpful beliefs. We don't even realise that they drive our behaviour and thought processes. These long-established, unexamined, and accepted as "the ultimate truth"s beliefs…

And when we become aware, we often don't believe that we can do much about changing them.

But we can. And it doesn't have to be hard.

Ask often, ask repeatedly, ask every day about everything:

Does this *serve* me?

If it does, great, keep it.

If it doesn't, great, let it go.

Here are a few statements. Read them and examine your own beliefs about them. Do you think that they serve you or they don't?

- I can't escape my genetics.
- I'm responsible for taking care of my parents.
- My child's path is my responsibility as a parent.
- I carry the pain of my ancestors.
- Change is so hard!
- It's hard to make money nowadays.
- Things are not going well in the world right now.
- Life is short.
- I can't change my past.

- Sugar is so bad.
- In order to be healthy, I need eight hours of sleep at night.
- My astrology map suggested a great year ahead.
- I'm in charge of my life.
- Change is easy.
- I can't sleep during the full moon.
- I can't exercise in the afternoon.

Does any of this serve you? Does any of this make it harder for you?

You can choose which ones to keep. It's your choice.

And you can choose to change any belief that doesn't serve you.

"THE 'SECRET OF LIFE'
IS BELIEF. RATHER THAN
GENES, IT IS OUR
BELIEFS THAT
CONTROL OUR LIVES."

Bruce Lipton

CAN YOU FORGET WHO YOU ARE?

We adopt numerous identities that define who we are and the way we think about ourselves.

"I am a mom…I am an extrovert…I am an Eastern European…I am a warrior…I get along easily with others…I am a good student…I am a procrastinator…I'm a lover of chocolate…"

Each one comes with certain characteristics and attributes that we, and others, based on their personal beliefs, attach to these identities.

In time, the more we build upon an identity, the more we bring it out, the more this identity defines us, and in turn, controls us. Our identity impacts our thoughts and behaviour; it shapes our choices. Soon, we live what we believe we are.

Can you forget who you are…
So that you can *build* who you want to be?

The past gave us an identity. But we don't need to carry it on anymore… unless we want to, to support our joyful creation, expansion, and growth.

The difficulty is that we would rather be in pain and suffer, than lose a familiar identity. It is what we know, and good or bad, we'd rather stick with it than shed it off. Plus, who are we without it? It comes from a deep need to stay consistent with how we define ourselves.

But once we remember that we were the ones building the identity in the first place, we hold the power to change it.

We can let it go or, even better, replace it with a new one that lifts us up and supports our journey.

Can you forget who you *are*?
So that you can build who you to *be*?

Who do you want to attach to your "I AM…"?

ASK INTERESTING QUESTIONS...

How can I afford to never work again?

How can I do more in less time?

How can I make this easier?

How can I work without using a computer for more than an hour a day?

How can I learn a new language effortlessly?

How can I work for only five hours a week?

How is abundance showing up for me right now?

How can I make this fun?

When we ask a question, the brain immediately starts looking for an answer, no matter the quality of the question.

We can ask close-ended questions that are easy and straightforward to answer, or we can use the power of the brain by asking more interesting questions.

When we ask interesting questions, our brain is gently forced to look for creative, out-of-the-box solutions. It generates options that we would have otherwise missed. It boosts innovation and creativity.

Compare the two:
"Can I afford this?" with "How can I afford this?"
"How can I increase revenue?" with "How can I increase revenue without increasing expenses?"

Take five minutes today and give this a go. Get a pen and paper. Think of an area in your life you would like to work on.

Write down as many questions as you can come up with, starting with HOW.

Brainstorm ideas and options. The rule is to never dismiss an option, no matter how silly or crazy it might sound. When you finish, you may choose an option you would want to explore further.

You don't have to have an answer right now. You can take a question with you and ponder it for a few days or weeks. Trust that the right answer will come to you.

Get into the habit of asking yourself interesting questions. The more you ask, the more creative you become. And even if a solution is too "crazy" or too "unrealistic", you have now brought it into your reality. It is becoming more and more real, and thus, more and more possible.

It is now in your vortex.

"I HAVE NO SPECIAL
TALENTS. I AM ONLY
PASSIONATELY CURIOUS."

Albert Einstein

Day 35

CAN YOU CHANGE?

Can you change your beliefs, your values, your preferences?

Can you change your thoughts, your behaviour, your habits?

Can you change your passions, hobbies, or career path?

Can you change who you are?

If you believe you can, you will.
If you believe you can't, you won't.

Most of us grew up being told that change is hard, challenging or even impossible.
"A wolf can change his coat, but not his character". This statement from folklore was frequently used in my childhood in regards to both vices and virtues. The story suggests that no matter how much you try, even though you can change temporarily and put on a new "coat", the change will not last. Deep down, you'll always be the same.

Most people find change hard, scary, and uncomfortable. With change, we invite the unknown, the unfamiliar. And, of course, we can provide many "facts" from our own lives to prove how difficult change can be.

But change doesn't have to be hard. It might feel like it, as even though we are in the process of change, there are many people in our lives reminding us who we are and what our preferences are. To many, the change feels threatening.

Take five minutes today to reflect upon your beliefs around change.

How hard is it for you to change a habit? How hard is it to change a pattern? A way of thinking? What about behaviour? Or personality? Or your personal reality?

What has formed your beliefs? Can you explore them more?

And...can you change them?

What I Love About...

I borrowed this from my wise friend Tracey (@tivanyshyn). Years ago, at an event we were attending together, I noticed how Tracey always used this phrase when she was introducing people to each other. She would say, "Sam, meet Didi. What I love about her is that she is…".

And then she will do the same for Sam while introducing him to me. I noticed how appreciative and beautiful this approach was to make people feel special, loved and seen.

A few days after the event, I took this powerful phrase and turned it into an exercise of appreciation for the most important relationships in my life. I sat down and wrote:

What I love about my partner is….

What I love about my mom is…

What I love about my child is….

What I loved about my sister is….

What I love about my nephew is…

What I love about my friend is…

What I love about myself is…

I would list as many things as I could think of in regards to the important people in my life.

It was very powerful and surprising, and I have been using it a few times a year ever since. It was powerful, because it made me aware of my own patterns of thoughts and concepts about significant others in my life. It made me aware of how much easier it was to list things about the children in my life versus the adults. It made me aware of how much easier it was for the brain to find things I didn't like versus those I loved. And it made me aware of how much more difficult it was to create a list of the things I loved about myself.

A very simple exercise, yet so powerful.

It requires us to focus on the positive aspects of everyone around us, and we know that what we focus on grows. It also brings awareness to how quickly and easily we are prompted to see the negative aspects versus the positive, especially with people with whom we have a long history.

What I love about …

Play with this today. Take ten minutes and list a few important relationships in your life. Write down a list of all the things you love about them.

See where it came easy. Observe where it was harder. Where was it effortless? What about the things you love about yourself?

Sit down with your observations.

What did you learn? What do you love about the people in your life, and about yourself?

"WHEN YOU FOCUS ON
THE GOOD, THE GOOD
GETS BETTER."

Abraham Hicks

CAN YOU STOP SAYING THE THINGS THAT YOU DON'T WANT TO BE, DO OR EXPERIENCE?

We are so attached to our stories, thoughts, judgements, and opinions, and we use every opportunity to bring them to life. We tell the same stories, we think the same thoughts, we act and react in a similar way to everything familiar, and we are quite happy to share with the whole world everything that doesn't work well.

"He never listens to me. I can't save any money. I'm not creative. I'm always procrastinating. I can't speak in front of a crowd. It's because of my upbringing. It is always so hard. I'm easily overwhelmed. I'm a terrible writer. I cannot cook. I hate my job. It's because I'm shy. I can't lose weight…"

It is easy to see the things that aren't going well. It is easy to see what doesn't work. And it's really easy to blame others or the environment. It is easy to blame our upbringing, colleagues, politicians, and life situations. And it is even easier to perpetuate the stories we are telling ourselves about the things that go wrong.

Can you stop saying it?

Catch yourself just before you are about to share what doesn't work. Bring your awareness to what you are about to say and remind yourself that you don't have to give it life.

Say "thank you" for showing up to remind you what it is that you DON'T want. And now focus all your attention on what it is that you want instead. Practise whenever you catch yourself wanting to voice out the things that you don't want.

In time, you'll create your reality based on the things that you want to be, do, and experience.

I DON'T KNOW

I don't know.

Yet.

I don't know how to make it easier YET.
I don't know who I am YET.
I don't know why I am here YET.
I don't know what to study YET.
I don't know if it's the right time to have kids YET.
I don't know if I will like it YET.
I don't know where I should live YET.
I don't know whether he is the right person for me YET.

Stop judging and blaming yourself for all the things that you don't know. You don't know them YET.

The Universe is not in a hurry. You are.

Soon you'll know. In the meantime, can you keep doing your best, keep doing what you are doing, without any resistance and fight?

And, of course, keep asking yourself all the questions to which you would like to find the answers. But without the urgency. As there isn't any. It's only in your head.

It's okay not to know.

I WISH

"I wish I hadn't yelled at him."
"I wish I'd been a better parent."
"I wish I'd told him I loved him."
"I wish I'd started earlier."
"I wish I hadn't taken it so seriously."

Regrets…

How many times can we punish ourselves for something we have done, or haven't done?

Many.

We feel bitter, frustrated, and sad. We suffer and blame ourselves, over and over again. We carry guilt and shame.

"I wish I had…
But I hadn't …"

What can I learn from it? What could I have done differently?

"I wish I hadn't…"
But I had…

You might find this interesting. In a study, conducted with Cornell psychologist Tom Gilovich, the types of regrets that have incredible staying power were those about what we *could* have done, not what we *did* do wrong.

Although we experience both sorts, studies have found that across cultures and demographics, it's regrets about *inactions* that haunt more of us for long periods. What can I change? Is there an action I can take to correct this? If yes, can I take it now?

If not, how can I forgive myself?

We don't have to fuel our regrets. We don't have to give them energy. It's up to us to reframe the situation, learn from it, and use regrets as a powerful tool to move us in the direction we want to go.

Can you catch yourself next time you are about to say "I wish I had or hadn't?"

What can you do to accept, change, or let go now that you are aware?

And remember to thank your regrets for showing you so clearly what it is that you want to change.

Day 40

Can You Dream It?

Can you dream it?

Today.

How do you want to feel? What do you want to experience?

Can you spend time dreaming today? Not planning, not creating lists with all outstanding tasks, and not thinking things through.

Time for dreaming. Where limits and restrictions don't exist. Where there are no budgets, scarcity, or logic. Where being realistic isn't welcome.

Can you dream it?

We forgot how to dream. When we tried, there was always something to remind us to come back to the real world. Soon, we exchange our dreams for settling into a familiar environment. And in time, we stopped trying. Instead of a joyful time, dreaming turned into an uncomfortable exercise that brought

us pain. As soon as we allowed the dream to come, the mind quickly reminded us where we stood right now. It gave us all the reasons why it wouldn't work or happen. It reminded us of our shortcomings.

No wonder we gave up. It felt easier. It felt safe.

What can help us start again?

We can start by seeing it as a creative practice. We can start by detaching ourselves from the dream until we feel comfortable taking it all in.

We can start by imagining that we are a screenwriter or a director of a movie, or a creator of a vision board, presentation, book… whatever feels comfortable. Imagine you are asked to create a movie and you are given all the budget in the world. No money limitations, no skills, abilities, or time restrictions, no location constraints. You can create anything that brings you joy.

What would it be?

Dream it freely - after all, it is only in your head. You don't have to make it real.

Give it a go.

Sit or lie down comfortably. Set the intention to dream freely, knowing that the right dream will come to you. Take seven slow breaths. Relax fully.

You are the creator of your dream. Who is in it? Where is it taking place? What do you do? How do you feel? What do you have?

Observe when a judgement arises and thoughts interfere.

Practise...

Keep creating your beautiful, imperfect story.

What do you want?

Dream it.

"IF YOU CAN DREAM IT,
YOU CAN DO IT."

Walt Disney

IF IT COMES FROM ME, I CAN HANDLE IT

If it comes from me, I can handle it.

It might not feel like it.

It might feel like it didn't come FROM me, that it came from the outside world. It wasn't ME creating it.

But it always comes FROM me. Yes, it might be triggered by events in the outside world, but the thoughts associated with these events, the disturbance created by these thoughts or what they unlocked in me, was created in me. It comes from me.

If it comes from me, I can handle it.

It might not feel like it right now. I might not feel able to handle it in this moment. But I would be able to…soon. If I wasn't able to, it wouldn't have come from me. And it always comes from me.

If it comes from me, I can handle it.

What a powerful belief to hold.

And how well it serves me.

NO ONE ELSE KNOWS
WHAT'S BEST FOR YOU

No one else knows what's best for you.

And you might feel you don't know either.

No surprise, with so much noise and clutter, with so many rules to follow, and with so many people around you who have long ago taken over your responsibilities.

It might feel easier to let someone else take charge, to know, to convince you of what's best for you.

And that's fine when it feels good to you. It's fine if you feel you are flowing with it. It could be that what's best for you, coming from the outside, is really what's best for you right now. As long as you enjoy it, it works.

However, be aware of all the other times when it doesn't feel good.

It doesn't feel good to *do* this, or *be* that.

All these times when you say *yes*, even though you really want to say *no*. When you do something because you have to, not because you want to. When you feel you're out of alignment, frustrated, stressed, overwhelmed.

It is during these times when it would be much more difficult to take back your power of "knowing". Because of all the other times when you let others decide for you.

For the sake of these times, please remember this:

No one else knows what's best for you.

Only you do.

YOU DON'T HAVE TO AGREE WITH ANYTHING I SAY

In fact, almost everything I say is not true.

It's true for me…

It might be true for a few others. Or many others. But being true to many others doesn't make it more true.

It is true for me because it reflects my beliefs and my understanding of the world right now. My view of the world is based on a complex mixture of my own experiences, conclusions, perspectives, and opinions. It includes parts of the collective consciousness of my community, area, and country.

It's really true for me (right now) and it might be true for you too. If it is, we will probably like each other more. But being my truth, doesn't make it a universal truth.
There are very few things that are true. All the rest is our perception of what's true.

You don't have to agree with anything I say.
I don't have to agree with anything you say.

I remind my son Mika regularly that he gets to choose what he believes in. He doesn't have to believe anything I say. He'd rather question and come up with his own truth than blindly follow mine.

Imagine how wonderful it would be if we were respectful of each other's truths.

How many battles could be spared! How much pain could be avoided if only we treated everyone's creation and worldview with respect and understanding?

You don't have to agree with anything I say.

In fact, everything I say is only true to me.

And it is true to me RIGHT NOW.

I can always change it, as you can too.

Be sceptical of everything, including your own truth.

WHAT IF I SAY YES TO EVERYTHING THAT HAPPENS?

I missed this opportunity that I was so looking forward to. **Yes**.

I missed the flight for this important trip. **Yes**.

I didn't get the job I wanted. **Yes**.

I lost money on this project. **Yes**.

I didn't get the house I dreamt of. **Yes**.

My "yes" might not be cheerful and happy, at least in the beginning. After all, I did not invite all these things that are happening and I don't like them.

But, rather than being disappointed and afraid, or sad and resentful, what if I choose to engage with whatever is unfolding in front of me from a place of yes! Yes, you... thing... that comes to me. If it happens, then it happens. I wonder, what's the gift in it? I am curious...

This way, I am allowing it to be as it is, dropping all resistance. I allowed it to be... for me.

What if I say yes to everything that happens?

It might not work, but I'm still going to practise.

Because...

What's the alternative?

I'M A PROBLEM SOLVER

Problems come my way…to be solved.

It's a big part of my identity, and I say it all the time, "Hey, I'm a problem solver. I'm really good at it."

After all, solving problems gives my Ego a lot of satisfaction. By now, everyone around me knows how great I am at solving problems. I can be counted on to resolve whatever needs to be resolved. I make things easier for others. I help! My Ego feeds on the rush of satisfaction and adrenaline. It grows stronger.

No wonder then, that problems come my way…to be solved.

I provide such a powerful point of attraction that is also amplified by that of the people around me, who know who to reach out to for solutions.

I am not going to say no. I am a problem solver. My Ego loves it!

I am quiet now.
I no longer say, "I'm a problem solver".

I don't look for problems to solve and I don't promote my great skills.

I'd rather have no problems to solve.

Yes, I'm still a powerful creator. I'm still a creative generator of solutions and engage with anything that brings me joy, even if I choose to label it a problem. But I'm conscious of what I put after "I am".

What about you?

You might love resolving problems, and that's great if it brings you joy, or if you derive great meaning while supporting your growth and expansion. But watch out for the many times when it leaves you depleted and overwhelmed. Bring your awareness to your point of attraction. That's all.

As Eckhart Tolle says in *The Power of Now*, "Just as dogs love to chew bones, the mind loves to get its teeth into problems."

Are you a problem solver?
Do you still *want* to be one?

THIS ISN'T A REHEARSAL

It's not a preparation for the main performance that is yet to come.

There is no getting ready.

It's my real life. It's me, living it right now. And it's happening now… not in the future.

There is no practising to get better at living life, hoping that one day I'll get there… somewhere. I'm already on the path.

There is no predetermined destination either. Sure, there is a direction, but I'm allowing the destination to change and evolve.

This is not a rehearsal for my real life-to-come…one day, in the future. One day, when I'll be, have, and do everything that (I think) I want to.

I remember vividly the day when I was in my early thirties, when the sudden realisation hit me like an ice-cold shower. I was living my life as if everything was just a warm-up for something big to come, a great preparation for my real life. In a brief moment, then and there, I realised I'd gotten it (somehow) all wrong. This wasn't a rehearsal. I've been living my real life all along.

The day has come… and part of it is already gone.

This is not a rehearsal. It's my real life. And I get to co-create with it in each and every moment that unfolds in front of me.

How wonderful that is!

TO ALL YOU KIDS, BIG AND SMALL, REMEMBER THIS

You're *not* responsible for your parents' happiness.

No matter how much it might be implied by them or by society, you are *not* responsible for their happiness.

It's never been your job to make them happy. It is not your job to make anyone happy but yourself.

Of course, you want them to be happy. You probably give it your best. After all, you came here to uplift, as we all did, to support and help. It's only natural to express it towards the closest people in your life, the ones that brought you to this physical reality. And how amazing it is when it feels good, joyful, and effortless!

But don't let yourself be convinced that your actions and choices are the reason for their happiness.

The chances are that, despite all your efforts, despite how much you try and modify your behaviour, they will be almost exactly as happy or unhappy overall as they were before you tried.

You're not responsible for their anger either, nor for their unhappiness. There is no debt that you need to pay back for being born and taken care of.

Of course, there is gratitude, respect, and appreciation. And without a doubt, there is so much beauty in co-creating and growing together, sharing life experiences.

But it's not your responsibility to change yourself, your personality, your behaviour or anything else, to make your parents happy. It won't work.

Every person has to learn to accept responsibility for their own happiness. You want it for them and you want it for yourself. But above all, you want it for your own children.

To all you kids, big and small, remember this:

You're not *responsible* for your parents' happiness. Free yourself from the heaviness of this duty, that has never been yours to begin with.

And when you have your own children, set them free too.

ɟ WANT...

I want to be really good at:

- Being happy
- Finding effortlessly many things to appreciate every day
- Bringing harmony and peace to others and myself
- Connecting to my inner wisdom and knowledge
- Thinking (frequently) better-feeling thoughts
- Feeling a sense of lightness and peace
- Laughing daily

Compare this to:

I want to be really good at:
- Public speaking
- Sales
- Copywriting
- Swimming
- Negotiation techniques

What if we set the feeling we want to feel as our goal, rather than the skill that will bring us the feeling we want to feel?

Sure, we might want to improve our sales or public speaking skills in order to make more money or have a greater impact on others, but ultimately, we want whatever we want because it will make us *feel* a certain way. We want to feel better inside. We want to be more at ease, lighter, more vibrant, and joyful. And we're pursuing the things that we believe will make us *feel* this way.

Why not set it as our primary goal to *feel* the way we want to *feel*?

People prefer to set SMART goals that are simple to measure and quantify. At best, these goals are objective and can be met within a specific time frame. "I want to be able to swim freestyle for twenty-five minutes by the end of the month." It is easy to confirm that the goal has been met.

Feeling happy or harmonious by the end of the month, on the other hand, may not sound like a very smart goal. No end result can be objectively measured. The journey, not the outcome, is the focus of this goal.

But isn't life about the journey anyway?

If I'm happy and joyful most of the time, and focused on feeling it, instead of focusing on becoming a better swimmer or the best copywriter in the area, wouldn't I be at the most amazing place anyway? It won't matter to me if I am the best copywriter or not. Why would it matter, if I am happy?

I might be afraid that I'll lose my desire to hustle with "feeling" goals, but what's behind this desire in the first place?

We tend to complicate anything that has the potential to be complicated. Why not take a break?

Give it a go. Set it as your primary goal to feel the way you want to feel.

What would be different?

"EVERYTHING YOU WANT
IS OUT THERE WAITING
FOR YOU TO ASK."

Jack Canfield

WHAT'S THE BEST THAT COULD HAPPEN...

If I go ahead with this project?
If I move countries?
If I go to this event?
If I invest in the training?
If I publish my work?

What's the best that could happen...

If I do nothing?
If I let it be as it is?

What's the best that could happen?

So often, we conceive a desire, a dream, or a wish, and then we quickly smash it before it has been given any chance to take off.

What if, with a little practice and awareness, we instead give it wings by focusing our attention on all the good that can come from it?

Our brains are hardwired to dwell on the negative, on what could go wrong, what would not work. It's been its job for millennia to protect us, to keep us alert to danger, to keep us safe.

Now that we are all aware of it, we can remember to be mindful of its programming. We can choose to focus on asking questions whose answers are dependent on a different part of our magnificent brain.

What's the best that could happen... if you go ahead?

What's the best that could happen... if you do nothing?

Now the mind will be looking for answers.

What's the best? What's the best?

In no time, it will creatively provide you with a list of things to play with.

And now that there is momentum, now that there is a foundation to build upon, you can decide what to focus further upon.

Keep asking.

What's the *best* that could happen?

Get your pen and paper ready and make it a little more real.

What's the best that could happen in regards to the decision you are making right now?

WOULD YOU ACT IN THE SAME WAY IF SOMEONE WAS WATCHING?

I took Mika to the playground. I don't recall the exact circumstances since it was a long time ago, but I do remember the realisation. It's been with me ever since.

Mika probably did or said something, and I addressed it in a way I wouldn't have, had we not been in public. If we were at home, just the two of us, I wouldn't have responded the same way.

Why then, did I do it there?

Because of the public. There was an unspoken social contract that somehow I'd consented to, and I was unconsciously complying with it. A contract that compelled me to respond to a situation in a way that society expects me to.

I was deviating from my values and ideals, otherwise, it wouldn't have bothered me enough to reflect, only because of the people who were watching.

I remember it made me think how strange we, parents, might seem to our children. The same situation could be addressed differently depending on who's watching. They must be perplexed, and in time, of course, they'll start copying us. They'll learn that while we're being observed, we should act differently.

To some extent, this is normal. We wear several "hats" and it's natural to act in certain ways in public, depending on the situation. We don't even have to think about it because it's ingrained so deeply.

However, when we depart from our own values and our own beliefs, in order to avoid being judged or criticised, we lose a part of ourselves, a part of our guidance system.

If I want to parent in a certain way, it's important to use my own values and beliefs as my compass. My conscious desire to be the parent (or the leader, the child, the partner) I want to be is my compass. Why give it away?

Take time to reflect. Do you parent differently when someone is watching? Why?

Do you act differently around your own parents when someone is watching? Around your partner, siblings, or colleagues?

If the answer is "Sure, it's fine, I wear a different "hat" when I am not alone", then great!

But if you feel that you are doing it for the wrong reasons, like other people's opinions and judgements, then it may be time to claim your power back.

YOU DON'T FIND IT...YOU CREATE IT!

You don't find happiness, you *create* happiness.

You don't find a purpose, you *decide* on a purpose.

You don't find meaning in your life, you *assign* meaning to your life.

Stop saying, "I am looking for happiness, I want to find my purpose or meaning in life."

As if they are hiding somewhere, and you need to find them.

You don't have to *look* for something that is up to you to *create*.

It's not hiding from you. It's simply waiting to be brought to life by you.

Plus, the more you look, the more you affirm to yourself that you don't have the very thing that you are looking for.

Relax.
There is no deadline. There is no single definition that fits a universal criteria for happiness, purpose, or meaning, no matter what old programming made you believe.

Remember that *you are* the powerful creator and you get to decide.

How wonderful this is!

TURN YOUR REGRETS INTO ACTION

"I wish I could go back in time to my twenties". Why?

"I would have started to take better care of my body right then."
"I wouldn't have cared that much about what they thought about me."
"I wouldn't have wasted so much time on things that didn't matter in the long term."
"I would have given it a go."
"I would have made more friends."
"I would have started to meditate."

Well.

Start now. Turn your **regrets** into **actions**, right now.

Because even if you could travel back in time in a magical way, chances are you would have done the same things you did. You've done the best you could have done with the knowledge you had then.

Now you have a different perspective and more life experience. You can see clearly what actions and beliefs would have been beneficial to your present *you*.

Start now. Whatever you wish you had started then.

Today. So that ten years from now, your future *you* won't look back with the same regrets.

Now that you know better, act with more *intention*.

Regrets are powerful because they can show you the path.

Today is a great day to start.

IS IT BASED ON FEAR?

Should I take this job?
"Yes, I fear I won't find another", versus "Yes, I want it."

"Shall I go on this trip?"
"No, so many things could go wrong", versus "No, it's not the right time for me."

"Shall I publish my work?"
"No, they would laugh at me and judge me", versus "Not in my plans now."

"Shall I deliver this presentation?"
"No, I'm not good at it", versus "No, it's not what I want."

I have been practising this for a few years now, every time I am about to make a decision on something that is still not yet clear to me.

Before I make a decision, I ask, "Is my decision driven by fear, or is it my true desire?"

If my decision is fuelled by fear, I explore it more before I go ahead, and, most of the time, I choose the opposite. I don't want my decisions to be based on fear, or avoiding fear, because I don't find fear to be a particularly good advisor in most cases. Plus, I know that my brain is wired to bring the fear out, and since this is beyond my control, I'd rather not even try.

I can dance with fear, but I can't shut it down. Therefore, I want to explore it instead, because if it goes unchecked, it will in no time drive most of my decisions, and, therefore, my life.

I ask, "Is my decision to do or not to do something, to say or not say something, based on fear?"

If I feel the answer is yes, now I know. The moment I bring awareness to the fear, I can now choose more consciously.

I would watch for that fear in any of my decisions. It might not always be present, but for the bigger, out-of-routine decisions, it will almost certainly be there but often masked When something is new to us, we fear it, and this is normal.

I would also look for it in decisions taken long ago, as well as those on autopilot, based on patterns and habits. It's interesting to revisit them and find out what motivated them. It doesn't mean I need to act on them, but bringing them to my attention can help me see things from a new perspective.

I'm so grateful for this question. If it weren't for it, I would have missed so many beautiful opportunities in my life to explore, learn, grow, and contribute.

Give it a go!

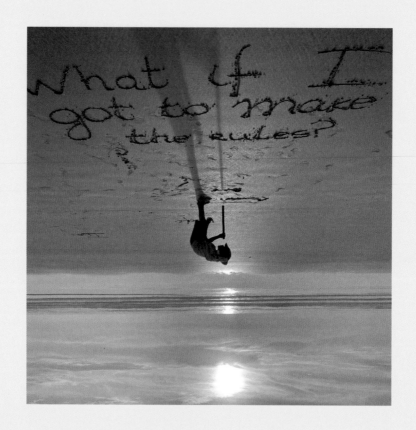

WHAT IF WE GET TO MAKE THE RULES?

The rules were already made for us. How to interact, what's acceptable, what to wear, what to say when, how to get married, what a relationship should look like, how many days off we can take...

The rules were already made for us, and we played by them, without even questioning them. We don't question because we forget we *can* question and because we often don't even know we are playing by a rule. We don't even see it as a rule.

We went to school and we followed rules that we didn't get to set, we didn't get to write. We were told to follow them, and we were praised when we did. We quickly learned, at this young age, that we'd rather not break the rules, because it would be harder for us. From then on, it was more of the same. College, work, clubs, friendships... We are rewarded when we agree and follow, and we are penalised when we don't. It's only natural that, over time, we forget to question. And we forgot we could.

What if we get to **make** the rules?

What if we decide on our work week, our vacation, our way of interacting, what creation is to us, what a fulfilling life looks like, our own definition of success, failure, and happiness?

We get to make the rules. But we aren't always aware of it.

And even if we are…

It might seem so much easier to play by the rules, rules written by others, than to create new ones.

Plus, it requires us to assume responsibility.

YOU get to make the rules. Will you?

It's up to you!

I WANT IT, BUT...

"It's not that easy."
"I don't know how."
"I don't have the resources."
"I tried before."
"Times are not good…"

I want it, yet I focus my attention on everything that won't let me have it.

I want it, but…

The "but" gives me all the reasons why I shouldn't try. Soon enough, it confuses me so much that I'm not even sure that I've ever wanted it at all. I'm now doubting my own desires.

It doesn't take long for this to become a habit. After the "I want," I just add a "but." I train my mind to focus on the things that hold me back.

What if, I change it to:

I want it, and…
This is what I'm going to do...

This is who I'm going to call…
These are the thoughts I'm going to think…

I want it, and…

Let me list all the things that support my "want", and let the momentum do its magic.

If I want something, I'm going to concentrate on that very thing that I want. The more I focus my attention on it, the more I bring it into my reality, and the more I allow my reality to catch up.

It takes awareness and practice, but it's well worth the effort. At the same time, I'm practising focusing my attention and providing wings to my desires.

Give it a go.

Substitute the "but" with an "and". Use the power of words and your wonderful mind, and let them work together.

What is it that you want… and?

"I TRUST THAT YOU KNOW BEST"

This is something I tell my son, Mika, regularly.

I trust that he knows best because he has his strong inner guidance system and he is still in touch with it.

Plus, who am I to know better? Sure, I have more life experience, but I have my own limitations based on my worldview. Who am I to override his own guidance? I can mentor and support him, but he has a much more powerful compass that he came up with.

When I meet someone who talks about their special relationship with their parents, I usually ask, "What do you think your parents did so well that made your relationship with them so special?"

"They trusted me", they would often say. "They frequently said that they trusted me."

As children, they felt empowered and connected, not afraid to express who they were.

"I trust you know best," I tell Mika.

And I remind myself, "I trust I know best".

I'm the only one who knows what's best for *me*. I'm the only one who can determine whether something will bring *me* joy or not, whether it's good for *me*, or important to *me*. I'm the one deciding.

And for a long time, I wasn't aware of it.

While I was growing up, no one ever told me that I had the answers within. The "answers" were given to me by much-more knowledgeable adults who knew better.

I wasn't encouraged to listen to my inner voice. On the contrary, my inner voice was often diminished and dismissed. In time, I believed it didn't matter, and I forgot I had my own powerful guidance system.

"I trust that you know best."

A message not only to my son, but to me and you too, in case we forget again.

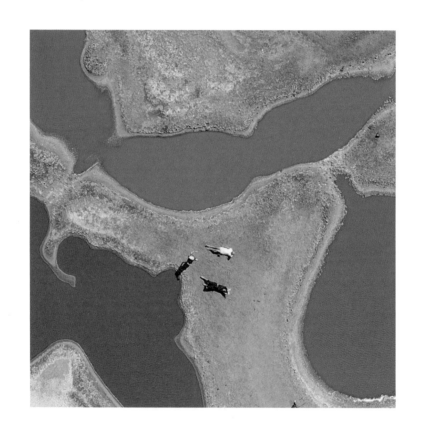

Day 57

WHEN DID YOU TURN YOUR PREFERENCES INTO RULES?

"I don't eat seafood."
"I only work out in the morning."
"I don't go to the opera."
"I only hire this type of person."
"I don't take night flights."
"I don't wear red."
"I only stay in hotels."

What will be different in your life if you break your own rules, or even better, have fewer rules to follow?

You might think you don't have a lot. It's awesome, if this is the case. But if you revisit your strong preferences, you might be surprised at how many you've already turned into rules, often unconsciously. You might realise how much power you've given them and how much they control your choices.

Sure, there are rules that you've created deliberately to support you. If they still serve you well, that's great! And if you keep in mind that you're in charge and revisit them when you feel it's necessary, that's even better.

But all these other rules, the ones that you might not even realise are now rules...take the time to examine them. Because of your adherence to those, you might have been limiting your life experiences and options.

Yes, on the surface, it seems easier to live by certain rules, and surely it is true for some. But how many times have you been disappointed and frustrated when life inevitably brought events that made you break your own rules? The more you are aware that these are just rules, likely based on preferences, the easier it will be to change them or let go of them.

The more rules we have, the less flexible we are - the less we let the flow of life take us places. The more rules we have, the less we leave space for surprise, spontaneity, and magic, the things that make life so wonderful.

When did you turn your preferences into rules?

If they don't serve you well, it's up to you to change them.

CAN YOU SEE THE BEST IN YOUR CHILD?

You might say, "Of course, this is exactly what I do." And you effortlessly list all the amazing things about your child.

And yet, on a daily basis, the chances are that you are giving your attention mainly to the things that they aren't doing right, the things that aren't going well. The chances are that you are nagging them much more than you're cheering them on. From the moment they are back from school, they hear mostly orders and commands.

"Don't do this, do that, don't say this, say that, don't leave this here, leave it there, don't eat this…"

If you draw a line and reflect upon the day that passed, you might realise that there was much more nagging and focusing on the things that weren't going well, the things that bothered you. There will be more disapproval than approval, more upset than calmness.

On top of that, we often worry about our children and express our concerns about them freely. We have the mistaken belief that the more we concentrate on the issues that concern us, the better equipped we will be to solve them.

We keep pointing out all the things that aren't going well and all the things we hope to avoid. Our attention is now laser-focused, and what we focus on grows. In addition, we openly discuss all that worries us with our partners, family, and friends. We make it even more significant. We make a story.

There is an alternative.

What if you see the best in your child consistently?

And then… can you do the same for yourself, too?

I CAN'T DECIDE

I don't know what's best.

Which one should I choose?
Is it worth it?

There are *small* and *big* decisions. Some won't make much of a difference, while others will. Some feel easier to make (what to eat), and some feel harder (which job to accept). And some feel like they are almost impossible to make from where we stand right now. They seem too overwhelming to deal with.

We think that the more time we spend on *deciding* something, the better our *decision* will be.

We weigh options, we make lists, we seek advice, and we make even longer lists.

And often, it feels heavy on us. The heaviness gets even worse when we linger in a state of not yet deciding. The more we linger, the more confusing it gets.

We were taught to seek information when making a decision. We were taught to be rational, to calculate risks, to consider pros and cons, and to analyse and examine. And we believed that there were wrong decisions and right decisions.

It's no wonder making decisions seems so difficult for many! We approach it as if we can predict an outcome, or control it. And we act as if there is only one right option.

What if, when I'm deciding, instead of using my mind and collecting information, I concentrate solely on one or two questions that I pose to my intuition instead? What if I simply ask myself, "Will this bring me joy? How will it make me feel?"

And then I listen for the answer, no matter what my mind's objections are.

My intuition is the shortcut. Depending on

how connected I am, I can hear a clear answer. Great.

Or no answer yet.
Great too. Despite what we believe, most things don't require a decision right now. I can do nothing and wait.

And I don't have to make any decisions so important that they overwhelm me. After all, I'm here to co-create with life, to play, to experience. Whatever I decide, it's **always**

the right thing. We assign great importance to far too many decisions because they often seem irreversible, and some are, but much less frequently than we think. We are afraid we'll make the wrong choice. And we get stuck in indecisiveness.

Much time and energy is wasted.

There is a shortcut, our inner wisdom.

Let's practise accessing it.

"YOUR HEART KNOWS
THE WAY. RUN IN THAT
DIRECTION."

Rumi

Day 60

YOU DON'T NEED TO PLAN IT ALL

You don't need to *know* the steps.

You don't even need to *know* what's next.

You can let the details show up through living your life, through actively engaging with what's unfolding in front of you.

When we plan, we use our minds. Our minds are both brilliant…and limited. The Universe is much more expansive and there are so many possibilities for something to unfold in a way that we can't imagine from where we stand right now.

Yes, we are *uncomfortable* with the unknown. Yes, we feel safer and more secure when we have a plan to follow for tomorrow, next month, or next year. But we don't realise that we are constructing our future from the past. We built it from our current perspective, which is mainly based on our past. We live in the same environment, we think the same thoughts, and we do the same things we did the day before. We follow patterns established long ago. And we plan using our limited minds.

Still, if you really love planning it all, and it serves you well, that's great! And you're

probably really good by this point at dealing with the frustration when things don't go according to plan.

But if you are ready to surrender to what life has to offer, if you are ready to co-create, then leave space for surprise, for magic. Be okay with not having a plan. Embrace living in the unknown.

Do more of what brings you joy. Serve with care and passion. Focus on helping someone today. Say "Yes" when you feel the answer is "Yes" and let the details crystallise. Engage with what's unfolding right now. *Trust.*

There is no need to figure it out in advance. You will while living through it.

And if you still feel a strong desire to plan, how about this:

Plan to *feel* happy, excited, curious, expansive, and joyful. Plan to *serve* with a smile.

And let the rest unfold in front of you.

———

A book I love on this is *The Surrender Experiment* by Michael Singer.

YOU CAME HERE TO PLAY

And somewhere along the way, you forgot it.

We came here to play, to have fun, to create, to experience, to co-create with life and others, to observe and participate.

There is no debt that we've accumulated in the past that we must repay in this lifetime. There is no suffering we need to endure for something we've already done before we showed up.

There are no rules that we set up before we came here and that we must now follow. We can change them at any time, at any moment.

There is no past life trauma that we are stuck with and must carry for the rest of our lives, and into the next.

Of course, there are predispositions, tendencies, and planetary alignments at the time of our birth that suggests we are more of this or that. In this body, in this place and time, there are personality traits and physical manifestations as a unique "me" and a unique "you."

However, "You" came as "You" so that you could express your uniqueness the way you want it now. Consciousness needs you… to expand through you.

You can choose to let go of the drama you've been carrying for so long at any time. You can choose right now, in this moment, to thank your ancestors and express to them firmly that all pain stops here. You can choose to drop the heavy stone (if you carry one) that they've been passing onto you generation after generation.

You can choose to say to your parents, "I love you and I am playing by my own rules. I hope you'll play by your own rules too."

You can choose to say to your kids, "I love you and I wish you to always remember that you have all the answers within. Remember, that you came here to enjoy your life experience."

You can choose to say to your mind, "I appreciate you so much, but I'm not going to listen to you anymore. I came here to play, and somehow I forgot about it. Please serve me well and remind me next time if I forget this again."

It's your choice. And you get to choose at each moment.

No one is really judging us. They are too busy judging themselves. And if we still think they do and then we pay attention to it, then we are becoming our own worst judges.

You came here to play.

IT MIGHT WORK FOR ME

It might work for me.

It doesn't mean it will work for you too.

Yet, we forget it.

We've forgotten it long ago, probably when we entered the school system. We were expected to be like the others, to learn in the same way the same things at the same time.

We are all different, and what works for *me* might not work for *you*.

It applies to almost everything, from exercise, meditation, recreation, healthcare, to play, diet, learning style, relationships.

We receive and give advice freely on what we should do, practice, or follow. We get frustrated when it doesn't work for us, and we try even harder. We also get frustrated when others don't take our advice… why wouldn't they? After all, we have already figured it out and are willing to share it.

We are all *different*.

It's great to test and try various things that have worked for someone else. And it would be amazing if they worked for you too! But keep in mind that they might not work in the same way, and it's up to you to bend and alter them to match your own individual needs.

It might work for me.

It doesn't mean it will work for you too.

And that's okay.

THE GRASS IS GREENER...ON WHICH SIDE?

It's up to you.

We may think that our neighbours, friends, family members, and colleagues, have it better than we do. We may think that they are luckier in this country or that country, or happier, more joyful, more successful, and have more opportunities. They surely must have it better! The grass is greener on the other side.

Not only is this hardly ever true, since we never know what anyone else is going through, no matter what it appears from the outside, but it is detrimental to our sense of fulfilment and happiness. By comparing ourselves to unknown other people, we diminish our life experiences and hinder our growth.

This is a huge waste of energy and time. Don't waste it keeping the grass greener on the other side. Spend it taking care of your own grass instead. It's not that hard because the moment you decide to begin, momentum builds and the Universe cooperates eagerly.

This is how it works. The more things you appreciate on your side, in your life right now, the more things to appreciate show up. The more you tend to your own grass, the better it grows.

And if you're still looking at the grass on the other side, why not use this opportunity as a creative exercise and fuel?

What is it that you like so much about their grass? Form a clear desire and follow it.

And make sure you appreciate their grass in the process.

HOW FAVOURABLE IS YOUR ENVIRONMENT?

I borrowed the concept from Montessori's philosophy and applied it to myself.

In the Montessori classroom, the Montessori teacher, who is more of a guide than a teacher, is responsible for following the child, observing, and carefully preparing the environment. It is the teacher's responsibility to create a favourable environment where the child can freely and independently explore, following their curiosity and at their own individual pace. Through careful observation, planning, and preparation of this rich and favourable environment, the teacher follows the child's interests, and facilitates their journey of discovery and wonder.

The "prepared environment" is one of the core components of Montessori philosophy. It is very important in supporting a child's learning, development, and growth. If a child in a Montessori classroom seems bored, agitated or frustrated, wandering without an aim for an extended period of time, the chances are the environment is not favourable enough. If it was, the child would have been busy working with and engaging with it. The teachers reflect on the environment daily.

A child is young and needs an adult to prepare the environment for them. But we are adults and we can take care of this ourselves, consciously assessing how to harness the power of a favourable environment for our own benefit, to support our growth and development effortlessly.

With or without Montessori, we all know how crucial the role of the environment is in our lives. And probably, naturally and intuitively, we have already built an environment that works for us. The thing is that what once was a favourable environment for our needs and desires at the time, might not be as favourable now. And we might have forgotten to reassess it and modify it.

For all you parents, please ask: "How favourable is this environment for my child? Does it support their learning and growth?"

And ask yourself regularly: "How favourable is my environment?"

"What are a few easy things I can do to modify and make it even better?"

IS IT WORTH IT IF YOU DON'T HAVE TO FIGHT FOR IT?

Most people feel that the harder it is to get something, the more worthwhile it is. The harder we fight or work, the greater value for the price.

Our culture is full of slogans such as:

- No pain, no gain.
- Push harder than yesterday if you want a different tomorrow.
- Anything worth having, you must fight for.
- Push until you get what you want.
- You grow through struggles.

These beliefs, in my view, have brought more pain and suffering than joy.

First, they aren't true - unless you want them to be.

Second, they programme us to value joy and satisfaction less (unconsciously) when something is easy to achieve. The word "easy" has a bad reputation. As if something was "easy", it wasn't that worthwhile. As if others would disapprove of you if things came easily to you.

Examine your beliefs in regards to easy and hard, ease and pushing.

If you think that what you want requires hard work, it will require it for you to achieve it. And if you think that you only grow through doing hard things and challenges, this is what you'll manifest.

It's up to you. Do what works for you, but bring awareness to it.

What I believe now is:

- No joy, no gain.
- The more I push, the harder it gets.
- The less I push, the easier it gets.
- It needs to be easy.
- The journey is more important than the ending.
- I grow through play, fun, and joy.

Choose your beliefs carefully. I know quite a lot of people who love it when it's hard; they love pushing harder and harder, and they feel they are getting stronger when they practise it. It works for them.

I used to be much like this. Until a few years ago, when I consciously chose not to be like this anymore. It works best for me now.

I catch myself when I push and I pause. I might continue, but now I'm conscious. Hard can be so much fun, when it's a choice.

It takes awareness to allow easy-ness in your life.

And if you like hard and it's hard for you, great.
If it's easy, great.

No need to bash one for the other. And we tend to bash the "easy" more, despite the pain of the "hard".

I can leave the effort to the Universe.

And as my consciousness grows, obstacles disappear.

""THESE MOUNTAINS
THAT YOU ARE CARRYING,
YOU WERE ONLY
SUPPOSED TO CLIMB."

Najwa Zebian

LET YOURSELF ENJOY THE RIDE

A young child paints for the pleasure of painting, not for the end result. It's the adult who, sooner or later, suggests to the child that they finish their painting.

The child doesn't care about finishing it because they finished it the moment they stopped being interested in it. They painted for the joy of painting and exploring. They were immersed in the present moment, in the journey, and didn't think of the previous painting, or the future painting.

The school system soon moulds the child to be more concerned with the reward, than with the joinery itself. Learning for the test result versus for the pure joy of learning.

Soon, the end *result* becomes more important than the *journey* itself.

We're willing to work and struggle for the things we believe will bring us happiness one day...when we get there. We believe that when we get to our end destination, it will be so magical and fulfilling that it will give the journey meaning and make it worthwhile. But the journey has been worthwhile right from the beginning.

Imagine aiming for the top of the mountain. You can't make it, because of the weather or something else that prevents you. Wasn't the trip still worth it?
The views, the attempts, the learning, the adventure.

And, of course, prioritising the journey doesn't mean living without a purpose or desire to aim for the things you want. It simply means focusing on the journey itself, and enjoying it no matter the end result. Because you are not doing it for the result. You are doing it for the experience and because you want to, not because it will bring you something in the future.

We often look too far ahead and miss the present moment. And in that way, we miss life itself.

Let's enjoy the ride, like we used to do when we were little kids. We know how. We just forgot.

"DON'T BEAT YOURSELF UP," THEY SAY

But, for most of us, it's hard.

We know that it's unkind to ourselves. And yet, we do it over and over again. This thing that I did, or said, or that thing I should've done or said.

I used to do it a lot. I would "pay" for the same "mistake" many times. I would go to bed, my mind endlessly running in loops over the same thing. And it brought guilt and shame.

And although I've been surrounded by people who are good at not doing it, I couldn't stop myself. It was stronger than me.

That was before.

I rarely beat myself up anymore. Not because there aren't things that trigger inner criticism (there are and that's okay), but because I'm so much better at catching myself at the moment and becoming aware of it.

I was a champion at "beating myself up". And now I'm (almost) a champion at noticing when I'm doing it, and I stop.

And if I can do it, anyone can do it!

How? A few things help me, depending on the situation.

I remind myself that it's in the past. Should have, could have, would have… doesn't matter anymore. If I can amend, I do it.

If I can't change anything now, if the opportunity is gone, then I'll do this. I'll become *curious*. I say to myself, "I wonder what the Universe is cooking up for me right now so that I missed this opportunity". And, because I trust the Universe, and that life works out for me, I keep this curiosity alive. I remind myself, "Remember, something even better is cooking up for you!"

And sometimes, when this is not suitable for the situation, I see myself as I see my son. Can I criticise him, over and over, for the same thing? Do I want him to do it to himself? Not at all. So why do I do it to myself? I also have an inner child! My inner being always loves me and accepts me. Always. It has a much broader perspective and understanding. When I am harsh on myself, I'm disconnecting from this source. This is unkind. No one deserves it.

Now, people may say that beating ourselves up keeps us morally in check. However, it's unhealthy when we build upon guilt and shame. That is never helpful.

But not criticising myself doesn't mean letting myself off the hook. Reflection matters.

Day 68

"I'M PROUD OF YOU."

I don't use the word "proud". Not for myself and never in regards to my child.

Ever since I studied neuro-linguistic programming, or NLP long ago, I've been conscious of the use of language. "Proud" never sat well with me, and I'll explain why.

Most people would use the word "proud" when referring to the achievements of their loved ones.

"I'm proud of my son for getting into this college."
"I'm proud of my kid for winning the swimming race."
"I'm proud of my child for building this business."

It is usually the achievement, the end result, that brings a moment of pride to the person's statement. But even if it's not the end result that is put on the spot, but the journey itself, similar to praising the process versus the end result, which I prefer, such as in "I'm so proud of her persisting on…, or trying, or…", I would still be cautious about using "I'm proud…".

I won't use it because this phrase includes my judgement and turns the attention to ME.

"I'm so proud of you, for doing/being….", suggests that I endorse something that I judge as great, that's why I'm proud. I prefer if my child does things not because of *me* and my opinion or the desire to please me as a parent, which all children have, but because it makes *him* happy. Who am I to give freely my opinions on his doing, which I do if I say "I'm proud of what you're doing?". In time, it can divert him from his own inner compass.

I may say instead, "Mika, I'm so happy that you are happy with….". But I won't endorse the action by inserting myself into the equation… as it has anything to do with me. People could argue that "I'm proud of you…" is the same as "I'm happy for you", but it's not. You are happy for them being happy with their choices, not for choosing or endorsing their choices.

I understand why people would say, "I'm proud of myself…". In this case, it is them, judging themselves, which is different from them, judging another person's achievement. It's better when expressed towards themselves.

As always, this is my own opinion. I share it in case you love words as much as I do and it resonates with you. If it doesn't, great! You know what works best for you.

Day 69

THE MORE...THE MORE...

The more I *give*, the more things are *given* to me.

The more good things I *expect*, the more good things *show* up.

The more things I *appreciate*, the more things are to *appreciate*.

The more I *seek*, the more I *find*.

But also,

The more I *struggle*, the more I *struggle*.

The more I *work*, the more there is to *work* on.

The more I see what doesn't *work*, the more it won't *work*.

The more I *criticise*, the more things I find to *criticise*.

The more I *complain*, the more things I have to *complain* about.

By now, we all know how the Law of Attraction works.

And yet, most of the time, we don't use its power.

If we did, we would remember,

to train ourselves to look for things to appreciate,

and to catch ourselves when we complain, criticise, or judge others and ourselves.

We will remember that it's up to us to guide our thoughts and focus our attention on what we want more of, not what we don't want.

It takes practice, but it's easier than you think it is.

Because once you are aware, you cannot be not aware. You can "fall asleep" again many times during the day, but as soon as you "wake up", you can practise.

And the *easier* it gets, the *easier* it gets.

It's like a wheel that has been pushed down the hill; it picks up speed and it's effortless. It can stumble and fall, but if you gently pick it up and push it again, guiding your thoughts and focusing your attention, it will speed up again.

Because the *easier* it gets, the *easier* it gets.

SHARE HOW IT FEELS...

Mika and I do silly things sometimes. We walk down the street, and suddenly we start moving our arms and legs as if we were dancing to a tune we don't hear or to some made-up song he sings. I always join him when he dances, and almost always it feels uncomfortable for a bit, especially when we are on a small street. We are marching, dancing, jumping…

A few weeks ago, we danced on a street in London. I followed Mika, I don't usually initiate these moments. Maybe it was because the street was narrow that I was more aware of the passing people this time. I noticed the brief discomfort that arose in me. Mika is not a toddler anymore, and it kind of looks strange… and I was aware of all the people looking at us.

This time, I decided to share how I felt with Mika. I wanted him to know that "his mom is feeling uncomfortable with this seemingly easy and ordinary thing, but she does it anyway". I said, "Mika, you know, sometimes when we dance on the street, it really feels uncomfortable in the beginning because I am aware that everyone is watching. But then I notice it and I get over it. I know it's fun for us and I am sure it sometimes brings smiles to other people seeing us."

He stopped and said, "WHAT? I can't believe it, I thought that only kids felt that way. I never thought that an adult could feel uncomfortable by doing that!"

I said, "And I thought the exact opposite! Kids are expected to be doing silly stuff, so they don't care as much as we, adults, do!"

Mika was genuinely surprised.
And I was even more surprised that he was surprised!

He believed that this feeling of discomfort was unique to children and not to adults. In his head, we adults are over it.

This episode reminded me to share the ordinary times when I am uncomfortable more often. As a habit, I usually tell him about times when I was afraid of something but did it anyway. I want him to grow up knowing that this is normal. But I didn't do it for the little, ordinary things.

It's great to share how we feel with our kids because sometimes they think that we are gods.

They think that we have it all figured out. When we share, we let them know that we never really do it, and that is okay.

Day 71

WHEN I FEEL DOWN, WORRIED, OVERWHELMED, OR SAD...

I sit with it and watch it. I don't suppress it, or avoid it, but I observe it instead, without labelling it or identifying with it. Most importantly, I let go of the effort to change it.

This is the important element and the one that made the difference - **no** effort to change it or fight it.

It wasn't like that before. I would always choose to suppress it, avoid it or divert my attention, doing anything that would help me not feel what I didn't want to feel. Sitting with it didn't feel like an option. I was afraid of it, thinking that I could literally drown in these strong feelings, or I could cross a door and there wouldn't be any coming back. Even ten days of a Vipassana silent retreat, meditating for fourteen hours a day didn't change it for me.

In the past few years though, this changed. I went beyond the diversion and the avoidance. I decided to be courageous enough to challenge this pattern. It worked for me and has brought me much peace. It's been so liberating.

Now, when I feel overwhelmed or anxious - which is much more rarely than before, I do this.
I sit with it. Detach from it and say to myself, "What a wonderful opportunity to practise!"

Resist nothing.
No effort to change it.
Just watch it.
Don't judge it.
Resist nothing.

And again: "What a wonderful opportunity to practise!"

Sitting with it, not trying to make it different, not giving it more power by fuelling it, has made all the difference.

Give it a go. It can make all the difference for you too.

Next time you feel overwhelmed, stressed, or down, or under the weather,

Instead of fighting it,
or trying to change it.

Can you detach?

And watch it?

You are not *it*.

You are the one who watches *it*.

It's liberating. It is a beautiful practice.

And if you've tried it, let me know how it worked for you.

The books that have helped me most with this practice are *The Power of Now* by Eckhart Tolle and *The Untethered Soul* by Michael Singer.

"YOU CAN'T STOP THE WAVES BUT YOU CAN LEARN HOW TO SURF."

Jon Kabat-Zinn

ΛM I WILLING TO LET GO OF THE DRAMA?

I may say, "Sure, I'm looking forward to it. I didn't create it, and never wanted it."

But even if this is true, we often keep it active, and we even invite it, whether we are aware of it or not. Why? Because it gives us identity. The Ego loves problems and drama!

The drama makes us feel alive. It often makes us feel useful, heard, and seen, and it brings more (wanted) attention to us.

Drama also requires a lot of energy and focus, and it is often easier to give it there, since it's familiar, than to take responsibility for our own powerful creation.

We are *addicted* to our problems. This is what makes it harder to get rid of them. As soon as we resolve one, another comes up. We need it so that we can feed off of it.

The solution requires us to not invest in drama, to lose our interest in it. And yes, it might not be easy in the beginning, but as soon as we stop feeding it, it gets dissolved.

Of course, people around us will try to draw us into their own drama. But it's up to us to participate in it or not.

Am I willing to let go of the drama?

The first step, as always, is to become aware when I catch myself engaging in or creating drama. I know, and I remind myself, that there is a reason for my human addiction to it. And once I'm aware, I can decide.

In the beginning, many decide to keep feeding it.

If you feed it, it will grow. And it might feel good (you are important, you get the attention). Or it might feel bad (guilt, pain, self-punishment), yet you can't yet drop it as it's familiar and it gives you identity.

But the more you engage with it, the more you feed it. How sustainable is this?

If you don't feed it, it will fade away.

Not engaging with drama doesn't mean being passive when a problem requires a solution. But the solution is never on the same wave as the problem, either. You can find a solution from a place of drama or a place of calm.

Am I willing to let go of the drama?

Take five minutes for quiet reflection: What drama does your mind create in your life right now? What if you let it go? Who would you be without it?

Day 73

DO YOU FIGHT OR COOPERATE WITH LIFE?

Probably both, depending on circumstances. In other words, when life is going on well, when the outer world is offering a lot of things to be happy about, you cooperate.

But when the outer world disappoints you, it's likely that you fight, you push against it. And the more it disappoints you, the more you push against it.

You *push* against the unwanted.

You *push* against your busy schedule, or the kids not cooperating, or the delayed train, or this project not working; you push against the things you can't control.

And the more you *push*, the more there is to *push* against. You simply keep it more alive.

Next time you catch yourself,

unhappy with what's going on,

complaining about the current situation,

nagging to the kids, or

telling the same unwanted story,

remember that you're *pushing* against it. Remember that you are fighting. When you *push*, you aren't cooperative. You aren't in harmony and you aren't flexible.

And when you *push* too much for too long, it becomes a pattern, a habit. Now it defines how you live. Your life feels like a constant fight,

instead of flow and ease.

Pause and ask yourself: "How can I cooperate with life instead? What if I stop pushing so hard?"

The more at ease you feel, the more you'll enjoy your life experience - the very reason you came here to this world…

I know some great "pushers". They live in a fight with what it is. The amount of energy wasted is never ever worth it.

Life is unfolding in front of them, for them, but they can't see it yet.

As powerful creators, our point of attraction matters the most.

THERE IS NOTHING TO WIN

There is nothing to win.

And there is nothing to lose.

It may not seem like it, because today's society promotes a win-lose mentality and teaches that winning is really important.

But the more aware you become, the more you'll realise there is nothing to win.

Likewise, there is nothing to lose.

We think that when we make it to the top when we get the prize, the recognition, the fame, there will be something special awaiting us that will suddenly give a whole new meaning to the journey.

We struggle to get there, we persevere, and we ascend in the hope of triumphing over it. And once we arrive, it doesn't take long for us to be disappointed once more, to realise that everything is the same and that the top is no longer sufficient.

The *win* has all along been in the *journey*, the win is us, being here, for the brief moment we exist. We've been told stories to get us hooked on looking up to the top, for the praise…

But there is nothing to *win*.

How liberating that is!

There is no battle to be fought, no coronation to be held, and no single reward to be won at the end of the journey. Because the journey doesn't end.

And there is nothing to lose in life.

So go ahead and do it. Take this trip, say the words, and do that thing. Play the game by your *own* rules.

CAN YOU FALL IN LOVE WITH IT?

If it's still on your plate and it's you who has to deal with it…

Can you fall in love with it?

Of course, the best thing would be to mostly (or only) deal with stuff and people that you love. And in the vibrational world we all live in, the more you practise your point of attraction, the more you'll manifest the things that you love.

But even if you are really good at practising, even if you are a master manifestor, there will be things you have to deal with that you don't like much, or at all.

You might not like filing your tax return this week or working on this paper. You might not like this part of your project. You might not like cooking for your kids every day. And you might not get along with this person on the team.

But the more you don't like it, the stronger the resistance is that you build.

If you can't change it, and if you can't avoid it,

can you *fall in love* with it instead?

Even if it's temporarily until you finish it or find another solution.

Because what's the alternative?

Doing it while hating it will only make it harder and more painful.

Doing it while loving it might bring you unexpected joy.

And because you'll be in alignment, the Universe will cooperate in the most magical way.

And if you still don't love it after that, perhaps now it's the time to find someone else who'd love it instead.

I AM NOT THAT IMPORTANT

I am not that *important*.

You are not that *important*.

In the immense Universe that has been around for 13.8 billion years, you…me, we all come and go in a brief moment. For an instant, we are part of life.

The world was here when we were born and will be here when we die.

We forget it all the time, and that's okay; it's part of our human experience as individuals. We place too much emphasis on our own importance, forgetting that there are millions of life forms around us. We, them, all… we are tiny specks in the grand scheme of things.

How much freedom comes from it, if you let it sink?

I am not that important.

You are not that important.

We are here for a bit.
Let's play together, let's enjoy the ride.

And no one else is more important either. There is no scale of "importance", making some more important than others. Your parents or other authority figures might argue, but this isn't the point.

We are equally *unimportant* from a larger life perspective. And we are equally *important*.

Nothing really matters much. And nothing is as serious as we make it.

And when we remember this, maybe we can relax. Because the "importance" weighs quite a lot.

Just remember:

I am not that important.
You are not that important.

"I DON'T LIKE IT!"

"I don't like it!"
"I'm sad!"
"It makes me angry!"

We've been conditioned to condemn the emotions that we don't want to experience. We suppress or avoid them, giving them even more power, because sooner or later, they surface. We resist, and they persist.

And we label what we feel. It's either good or bad, amazing or horrible. Of course, we want to feel more of the good feelings and less of the bad feelings. And in the vibrational Universe we live in, this is quite possible, the more we learn to guide our thoughts and elevate our vibration.

But feeling angry, sad, or fearful is part of our emotional range; it's part of the contrast we came here to experience. We can't not feel these, while we are in a physical body.

So what?

We don't have to turn them into a story that defines our overall experience. We don't have to label them as negative and become "stuck" in them. We don't have to suppress them or avoid them.

The best we can do is this.

"I am sad."
"I am angry."

So what? What's wrong with that?

I can sit with it and let it go. It is just an e-motion, energy in motion.

There will be times when I'll be sad, angry, or afraid.
There will be times when I'll be excited and joyful.

I'll do my best to reach out for the joyful times. And if I'm to make a story, I will make a story out of these.

But the rest is still a part of life. It comes and I can let it go.

It's a practice.

The ultimate liberation comes when we don't get wrapped up in our preferences, neither towards the good feelings nor the bad feelings. We just watch them come and go, like a wave, without identifying with them.

This is what I imagine inner peace to feel like.

Day 78

"HELLO, FEAR!"

I greet it every time it shows up.

"There you are."

I know that by recognising and acknowledging it, I'll make my life experience so much richer, and lighter. If I ignore it, push it down, avoid it, dismiss it, or get frustrated by it, it will soon take the driver's seat. Many of my life decisions will be influenced by it, and I may not even be aware of it.

Fear will almost inevitably show up, one way or another, in regards to the many important and less important things in my life. Raising my son, caring for my family, working on this project, the trips I go to, the initiatives I undertake.

And that's okay.

We were taught to be ashamed of fear, to do our best to overcome it, to even fight it. We admire the courageous, wrongfully believing that they don't experience fear, that they are truly fearless.

But fear is almost always present, one way or another. It has its own evolutionary role to play and is with us for a reason.

We don't have to get mad at it.

Or let it overcome us.

I often ask, as part of my decision-making process, is this coming from a place of fear?

If I know that fear will often accompany me in my life, I'd rather treat it as a friend, one that I don't need to welcome often, but when it shows up, I greet it. I say hello and recognise that it comes for a reason.

And then, I can make my choice. To act as I want to act, no matter what it tells me.

Because I don't find fear to be a great advisor.

But I choose to get curious about it.

"Why do you come? What do you have to say?"

I greet it, *recognise* it.

Thank it and *release* it.

Until next time.

NOTICE THE SIMPLE PLEASURES

Taking off your ski boots after a long day of skiing…
Wrapping up a box of chocolates to give to a friend…
Singing alongside the music on the radio…
Helping a new mom with her stroller up the stairs…
Petting the stranger's dog at the cafe…

We can so easily miss these little, ordinary moments.

We assign more value to the extraordinary, to all these things that we consider rare, hard, or unusual. And that's understandable because the extraordinary is different. We notice it, we might strive for it, but in our pursuit of it, we frequently lose sight of the ordinary moments that make up the sum of our lives.

The thing is that all moments matter. But our racing minds, so focused on the future or the past, do not register most. We sleepwalk through the day, rushing to get somewhere, rating our life experiences and judging negatively all that we consider "not good enough", or mundane. We develop scales upon which we rate our life moments.

And only when life offers us situations that shake us in some way, only then we suddenly appreciate the little ordinary moments. We realise that they do matter. And when things aren't going great, we are looking forward to some simple, ordinary time.

Simple pleasures…

Taking a shower in the evening…
Brushing your hair in the morning…
Laughing with your child…
Sipping cacao….

What if you practise bringing awareness to these moments every day?

WHAT IF WE GOT TO LEARN FROM OUR KIDS?

What if we got to learn from our kids?

Because:
Children look for ways to feel good.
They are clear on what they want or don't want.
They are eager to share their wants and dreams.
They don't feel they need to explain why they want something. They want it simply because they want it.
They freely express their emotions.
They look for things that bring them joy without judging them.
They look at life with wonder.
They don't care about the end result.
They can do something for a long time, or for a few moments. It doesn't matter.
They change their interests as much as they want to.
They laugh hundreds of times a day.
They are open and direct in their communication.

They don't care what most people think of them.
They follow their intuition.
They believe in magic.
They are quick to forget.
They don't wallow in self-pity, guilt, and blame.

How wonderful is this?

What if we remember who we once were?

And if we can't just yet, maybe we can adopt a more child-like approach to life in the meantime.

And for those of us with kids at home, we can set up the intention to observe them more and interfere less.

What if we got to learn from our kids?

"IS IT ALLOWED?"

This is a phrase I've heard a few times from my son Mika since he went back to school this year.

It struck me, because it was new in his vocabulary and I'm very aware of our use of language.

Upon reflection, I realised I shouldn't have been that surprised. "It's not allowed" is frequently used in situations where people are expected to follow rules that were designed to make life easier, safer, and more predictable, often for those who wrote them.

And "it's not *allowed*" is still softer than "it's *forbidden*", which I grew up with under communist rule.

After Mika said it a few times, it made me reflect upon its long-term impact on our actions and beliefs.

Whom am I asking for permission? What is the cost of letting someone else decide whether or not to allow something? Where and what do I restrict in my life?

I AM allowed…

To push boundaries.

To think differently.

To be part of the rule-writing process.

To say what I think.

To dream beyond my current reality.

To question or to disagree.

To change my beliefs.

To focus on things that bring me joy…

Are you?

And who is the one that doesn't allow it? Parents, community, family, old beliefs?

It could be any. We were not initially allowed something, we were taught to follow the rules. And even though we grew up and it was up to us to define the rules, we kept living from a place we knew. It was safer.

But in the end, it comes down to me, and you.

You are the one that does not allow yourself to dream bigger, to try new things, to choose new beliefs, or joy over what others say is important.

Remember this story? A little elephant was tied up to a post. He was only able to circle as far as the rope would allow it. He grew stronger, and despite the fact that he might easily have torn the rope, he didn't. He kept walking within the circle he was familiar with.

The one who doesn't allow it **now** is not the school teacher, or this organisation, or that government, or this authority.

The greatest "non-allower" is **you**!

How liberating to know it!

Now you can start allowing *yourself* all that you desire, and beyond.

Because it's up to *you*.

You don't need to ask for permission.

You *are* allowed.

"CHANGE ISN'T MADE BY ASKING PERMISSION."

Seth Godin

WHAT TYPE OF PARENT DO I NEED TO BE FOR MY CHILD?

It matters how we show up in our relationships with our kids. We have our own individual preferences, traits, and desires and, of course, they might be different from those of our children, but we often forget.

And we have, no matter what we say, certain expectations of our children. It's difficult not to have any. There is nothing wrong with having some general expectations; we transmit vibrationally anyway, through the energy field in our relationship. It's wonderful to have high standards and expect the best for them. But it's important not to have a strong attachment to these expectations and not to put them on our kids.

Our children are different from us. Yes, we may love to "find ourselves" in them, in their actions, in their ambitions, predisposition, or personality. Our Ego loves the similarities. But they are not our extensions. They come with their own unique personality and unique point of attraction, *through* us, not *for* us.

They were born into a "different everything". They came at a different time, with different vibrational energy, and a different vortex, that, according to Abraham Hicks, goes much faster than ours. And the best we can do is to honour these differences in the way we show up for them.

You might be someone who loves rules, structure, or planning. And yet your child can exhibit a preference for the exact opposite. Would you impose your preferences on them? Or would you cherish and support theirs?

This question has helped me a lot in my parenting journey.

"What kind of parent do I need to be for my son?"

Of course, I don't need to change myself or my personality. That won't make me a good role model anyway. But I could be a certain type of parent who supports his individual development. Individual... because every child is unique. We can't have one size fit all in regards to our children, and yet, we often try... because we aren't aware.

What if we observed our kids with full presence, in a way that allowed us to get to know their essence? Only then we can truly follow them.

What kind of parent do you need to be for your child?

It's Up To Me

I want to dream. And it's up to me.
I *create* my own reality.
I want to fly, and that's okay.
As I will *not* choose to fly away.

I can be grounded, and that's fun too.
Cause I know that I can always review.
I can be free, completely free.
And this is what I choose to *be*.

I may want to cry. Let it be.
I may want to shine, or disagree.
I may want to hide far away.
Until I feel like coming back to play.

I may want to dream, all days and nights.
About knights and castles, and battles and fights.
About audacious inventions and highlighted life,
Or anything else, for which I might strive.

I know very well, that I can have it all,
For I am the one who sets the goal.
I am the one who can dream and create,
And you can too...

Just don't be afraid.

I love you, life, you're full of adventures
I am now off, to set my intentions.

WHAT'S YOUR WHY?

Why do you do what you do?

Because I want to.
Because I signed up for it and I'm following through.
Because I don't know what else to do.
Because it's what I have been doing for a long time.
Because it makes sense.
Because I love it!
Because I thought it would be fun.
Because it's good on my resume.
Because they told me it was the right thing to do.

Because...

Why do you do what you do?

Whether it is about your job, your hobby, your daily routine, your parenting style, the way you communicate, or the projects you choose.

It's worth reflecting on this question.

What needs to go? What would be a good addition?

How deliberate is your creation?

Why do you do what you do?

Does it bring you joy?

Day 85

Would you rather welcome it or resist it?

It's up to you.

Change is constant and most often uncontrollable, and it doesn't require our permission.

Would you *welcome* it,

or *resist* it?

Of course, I would love to welcome the change that I seek (although I'd probably unconsciously resist this one as well).

And, I would rather not deal with the change I don't like, I didn't plan for, and it seems beyond my control.

My mind would always hold strong preferences **for** and **against**.

But the more I resist the change I dislike…the more I push against it, the more powerless I'd feel. The more energy I spend, the stronger the resistance will become.

What's good about it?

I better welcome it instead.

And look for the gift in it.

It's not the changing world that creates the pain, it's my resistance to it.

Then I ask…

How can I drop the resistance to change.. and allow it to be?

I keep bringing my awareness to it. Not to the change per se, but rather to my resistance. What's behind it? What's the fear?

Then I can let it go…

and turn my attention to how I want it to be instead. I can focus on the change I want to see and be part of.

And how wonderful it would be, if I could let go of my attachment to it.

CAN YOU SEE IT FOR THE FIRST TIME?

Without the labels, the long-ago constructed stories, the expectations, the identification?

Without affirming what it is that you liked or didn't like before in regards to it, without the preconceived notions.

Can you?

Can you see your mom as if you've never seen her before, as if you met her for the first time, without automatically applying all the usual opinions you hold about her?

Can you listen to them speak as if you've never heard them speak before?

Can you look around the room with new eyes, as if you've just awoken in an unknown place?

And,

can you see yourself without the layers and the labels that the Ego has constructed long ago?

Probably we can't. Yet.

But the more we practise, the better we get at it.

It takes *intention* and *awareness*.

Intention to be willing and open to "seeing it for the first time", with a sense of wonder and inquisitiveness, to give it our full presence.

Awareness to catch ourselves in the moment when our minds inevitably drift to quick judgements and labels.

This practice takes a lot of courage, because the Ego won't like it. The Ego loves its opinions, and it has developed strong attachments to the reality it has constructed. It won't give them up easily.

Why do it then?

Because of the expansion that comes from this practice, because of the presence in the moment, and the magic and fulfilment that comes from seeing the world "for the first time". Because of the infinity of choices that will open up in front of us, when we choose to go past our conditioning.

Can you *see* it for the first time?

The trees, the plants, your child, the clouds, the food on the table, the man on the street, the car, the pavement, the piece of wood, your hand…

What's going on within you?

YOU CAN'T GET IT WRONG

You can't get it wrong.

"But I did, and I still do, often."

"I've been wasting my life."
"I dislike my job."
"I keep overeating."

Or,

"I chose the wrong career."
"I prioritised the wrong things."

On and on...

Still, you can't get it wrong.

If you now have the awareness that this was the wrong thing, the wrong choice, then you possess powerful knowledge. Now you know it was (or it still is) the wrong thing for you, and you can do something about it.

From a higher perspective, almost nothing ever goes wrong. Whatever happens, it happens to help you clarify what it is that you don't want so that you can get more clear on what it is that you do want instead.

And there is nothing you could have ever done wrong.

Because if you knew better when you did it, you would have done better. You've done your best with what you had or knew at the time.

What you've labelled as "wrong", was just a signal, showing you, telling you, that this didn't feel right, that it takes you out of alignment.

How powerful this is.

So next time you catch yourself judging something you've done as wrong, remember that you can never get it wrong.

It's now up to you to pay attention to the "signal". What would you have rather done instead? What would you do next time?

Good to know.

I love this quote from Abraham Hicks: "You can't get it wrong because you never get it done."

It's never done, because you get to choose at each and every moment.

CAN YOU REMEMBER TO FORGET?

The thing that he said that hurt you.
The mistake you made, that keeps haunting you.
The guilt that you carry with you from your childhood.
The shame that sneaks up on you, uninvited.
The event that made you feel insignificant.

Can you remember to forget everything that doesn't serve you? The stories that your mind chooses to keep alive and "on repeat", over and over, making them stronger and more powerful.

Remember to forget the beliefs that keep you acting and feeling small and limited; the advice from well (or not) intentioned others that might not work for you; the responsibilities that were never yours to take on in the first place.

Can you *remember* to *forget*?

And if you can't just yet, then let them come up. Face them. But make it a practice to turn their volume down, each time a little bit more, until they only whisper.

Make a vow to take away their power by not voicing them out loud again and again, by refraining from discussing them with others, by keeping them silent.

And every time they creep back into your mind if you are not ready to let go of them just yet, can you sit with them instead, and bring them to light. They all served a purpose.

Can you remember to forget?

All that doesn't serve you.

The more aware you become of what it is that doesn't serve you, the easier it will get to let it go. It all starts with *awareness*.

CAN YOU REMEMBER TO REMEMBER?

That you came here to enjoy and play.
That you are a powerful creator.
That you have all the answers within.
That you came equipped with a perfect inner compass.
That you are endowed with great wisdom.

Can you remember to remember who you really are behind the mask? Remember what a precious gift your life is, no matter how you feel today.

Can you remember to remember how abundant the world you live in is, how full of riches, wonders, love, and light, no matter how difficult it is to see it at times?

Can you remember to remember that you've been through a lot so far, and yet you made it, bruised and tired, and while it may not make sense right now, it will one day soon?

Can you remember to remember that you are always loved and accepted just the way you are, no matter how hard it might be to believe it right now?

Remember to remember all the wonderful moments that you've had and you desire to have in the future, all the things that make you laugh, all that brings you joy.

Can you remember to remember that you could be and have it all, all that you could ever wish for or it wouldn't come to you if you didn't have the capacity to make it happen?

Can you remember to remember why you came here?

What for, if not to grow, expand, and enjoy, on your own terms?

You forgot it all, growing up. That's okay.

Because you **can** remember. And there will be so much joy and happiness in remembering.

There are infinite possibilities that lie in front of you in this beautiful, cooperative, constantly expandable Universe. And your being is needed to support this expansion, although you might not be aware of it just yet.

Remember to remember…

CAN YOU DROP THE "-EST"?

The smart-est, the fast-est, the happi-est, the nice-st, the bigg-est…

Can you imagine how different your life would be if you dropped the ever-present comparison with them?

From early on, we've been programmed to compare. Our parents compared us to our siblings and other children. Our teachers compared us to classmates based on behaviour, attitude, and test results. We went to work and we were compared to our colleagues.

Now, there is no need for anyone to compare us anymore, because we do it ourselves quite well, all the time. We constantly evaluate ourselves in comparison to someone else, to their skills and abilities. We compare our revenue, growth, ratings, number of followers, and number of awards.

The Ego would always want to compare. But the heaviness comes from the judgement that follows each comparison. In most cases, we judge ourselves as being less than others. Sometimes, we judge ourselves as better than others and the Ego truly loves it. Either way, we pay a price for it.

The more we compare ourselves to others, the more distracted we are from our own dreams and wishes. The more we turn our attention to them, the others, the more we lose our connection with our desires. Soon we will be going for the things that others value.

We came here as powerful creators. Not as competitors. Not as someone who is better or worse than anybody else.

Some may think that comparison is useful. It pulls you up, it motivates you to pursue something, it pushes you to want to do better, to progress, to grow.

If this is how you feel, and it works for you, great. If it stimulates your own ideas and desires, great. As always, whatever serves you well, make sure you keep it!

But if you feel that comparison puts you down; if you realise that you follow external motivation for the sake of yet another -"est" then you might want to bring awareness to this practice. Because no matter how much you push towards the next title, even if you get it, soon it won't be enough.

Comparison is never-ending. There is no winning in this game.

The only comparison that is worth mentioning is this:

"I am here. I'm heading there. This is my progress."

CAN YOU DARE TO BE YOURSELF?

And why is this even challenging?
What has happened to us? What makes it so difficult for many to be themselves, so much so that we need *courage* to be able to embrace the fullness of who we are?

Look at the little children. Proudly expressing their personalities. Saying "yes" and "no" as it pleases them. Drawing a few lines and calling it a rocket. Sharing their toys if they feel like it. Wanting just because they want. Being truly themselves…

Children don't need *courage* to show who they are. They are freely expressing their personalities and individualities, their tendencies and desires.

They need *courage* to do other things that are important for their development, like exploring the unknown world. But they don't need courage to **be** themselves, because **being** themselves is the easiest thing in the world!

We were all like this once. And then we began growing up. We were assigned expectations and rules for just about everything. How to greet, how to wait, when and how to talk, how to address your parents and grandparents, teachers and strangers, and how to participate in society. We were told off when we didn't act as prescribed, which was usually quite often and soon we began to forget who we really were.

We forgot what we loved doing, we dismissed our interests, and we became cautious about expressing ourselves as we were often judged.

And by the time we became adults, we got confused. We've been practising being someone else for so long that we've forgotten who we **really** were.

It's up to us to *remember*.

Sure, we now need courage to start with. But as soon as we intend to dare to be ourselves, as soon as we take the first step, the momentum will get us going on a fast track. We know who we are. We have just disconnected from our knowledge. Deep down, we feel it, and as long as we give it space, it will become more and more prominent.

Can you **dare** to be yourself?

You can start by asking yourself every day about anything you do: Does this bring *me* joy?

Does it bring joy to *me*, not to my child, my spouse, my parents, my boss, or my friends?

Following *your* joy is the fastest way to reconnect with your true self.

Do you *dare*?

WHO IS IN CHARGE?

My parents.
My kids.
My partner.
My government.
My life circumstances.

Who is in charge?

It's tempting to outsource responsibility
for my actions, behaviour, attitude, and life
circumstances to someone else. After all, it's
logical.
"I had this childhood."
"My country imposed these restrictions on
me."
"My grown-up kids are responsible for me
now, as I was responsible for them before."

It makes sense. We are constantly intertwined
with others and the environment, and we can
truly feel, often, that everything is outside of
our control.

After all, I didn't want it to happen this way. It
wasn't my choice. It's not my fault.
Well, the truth is that it doesn't really matter
whose fault it was, and looking for someone or
something to blame only impedes my growth
and life satisfaction. Also, it doesn't really
matter how bad it was. It doesn't really matter
how hard it was. It was…it doesn't need to be
in the future.

What matters is, who is in charge now?
Are you?

Sit with it. What's the immediate answer that
comes to you?
Who is in charge right now?

The difficulty comes if you have been
practising not being in charge for a long time.
Then it's hard to believe that you can be.

Often, not being in charge might feel much
more effortless. After all, you are not assuming

additional responsibilities. You don't have to figure things out. It's easier to follow.

If it works for you, as always, that's great.

But if you feel that you aren't in charge and you hold resentment, then it might be time to remind yourself of this.

It's up to me to take the wheel. It isn't up to my boss, my partner, or my parents. I take responsibility for my actions and attitude. I take responsibility for my choices, thoughts, and emotions.

And I take responsibility for my beliefs.

I am the creator of my own experience. Not you. You do you. I'll let you assume full responsibility for your own life.

I am in charge of my own life.

How wonderful this is!

And for all the parents here, how amazing it is to know that you showed your kids the magnificence, the deliciousness, of being in charge of their own life. Set them free. It's one of the most precious gifts that you can give them.

"YOU CANNOT ALWAYS
CONTROL WHAT GOES ON
OUTSIDE. BUT YOU CAN
ALWAYS CONTROL WHAT
GOES ON INSIDE.."

Wayne Dyer

WHY?

When I studied neurolinguistic programming and coaching years ago, I remember the emphasis on asking good questions.

In NLP we think a lot about language and its impact on people.

For example, it is always better to ask open-ended questions starting with *how, when, what* because you can get an unexpected and creative answer that is not determined by the limitations of the question itself. A closed-ended question requires a "yes" or "no" answer and has already put you in a box. You have only two choices to answer, and you might not feel your answer fits either.

The word *why* caught my attention. Before, I never questioned the usage of *why*; I thought that *why* questions were amazing; they were looking to figure something out, to learn, to know, and they can be, in certain cases.

However, why questions can be quite provocative. People who are asked *why* feel on the defensive. *Why* may come across as aggressive.

Why did you do that?
Why didn't you tell me?
Why are they not calling me?
Why are you doing it this way?

Even when we ask ourselves.
Why did I eat this? Why didn't I go?

A question that starts with a *why* demands justification from the person answering the question. Instead of genuinely looking for the answer, the recipient may instinctively go on the defence. This might have something to do with the way we've been raised. *Why* can put us in an inferior position, where we have to explain ourselves.

Why probably wasn't meant to be an attack question, yet most people will perceive it as such. It will evoke an emotional response. Good leaders avoid using it overall. I'm quite conscious of its use as a parent as well.

A much better question to ask starts with *what* or *how* instead.

What made you do that? Tell me more…
What prevented you from telling me?
What happened, I wonder. They haven't called me yet.
What's behind your way of doing it? Tell me more.

How come I ate that?

With these questions, we come from a place of curiosity. We ask so that we can learn. They invite reflection.

And we will learn much more than if we simply asked *why*.

Try it.

How often do you use *why*? How do you feel when you're asked *why*?

Why?

"WHEN I SPEAK, YOU
MUST NOT LISTEN TO THE
WORDS, MY DEAR. LISTEN
TO THE SILENCE."

Anthony De Mello

LET IT SHOW YOU

"Life is a simple affair," Michal Singer once said.

"It unfolds in front of you and you engage with it."

I am doing my best to live by this truth.

It unfolds, I engage. It unfolds, I engage.

Why should I wait for it to unfold? After all, as a powerful creator, I am the one who creates my own reality. Why should I wait for life to shape it for me?

I see it this way. Allowing life to show me, to unfold in front of me without attaching myself to my preferences and expectations, means I am co-creating with life on a much larger scale. In my dreams, I'm bound by where I come from. I have certain beliefs, ideas, knowledge, preferences, abilities, and my wishes and intentions will reflect this mixture. I can be very creative and I can have a beautiful and vivid imagination, yet I'll always be limited by the mind.

Life can have much bigger dreams for me. Bigger in the sense of beyond my imagination. It's a magnificent partner in co-creation. If I let it show me by engaging with what is unfolding in front of me, I surrender to the flow of life. Life is so much bigger than me. Why not

practise letting the flow take me to places that I could never have imagined?

It might feel uncomfortable at first. To let life unfold in front of you means to live in the *unknown*, to embrace it. It can be scary. But it is a beautiful practice in surrendering and acceptance, and beyond it, lies freedom.

Letting life show me doesn't mean I don't have desires or intentions. I still get to choose my thoughts and attitudes and what's important to me. We came here to play, engage, dream, make things happen, grow, and expand. There is no one single definition of how we express all of this.

Letting life show me means keeping an open mind. Be willing to drop preferences. Engage with the unknown and let it guide me. Let the flow take me places. Don't hang onto expectations. Be flexible. Flow.

Ultimately, we all came here to enjoy and share our experiences with other powerful creators. And it doesn't really matter how we do it, as long as we are free and let others be free too in the way they choose to express themselves.

Let life show you.

Will you?

Day 95

ꓳon't push it

I practise this and it has made a big difference in my life.

I don't push too hard. I am on the watch. I'm getting better at catching myself when I fall into push mode.

I used to believe in pushing. I used to believe that pushing through things made me stronger and better prepared; that everything worthwhile lay behind the push line. It was worth it because it was hard. If something was a struggle, great, let me deal with it. After all, all growth comes from pushing, I believed.

I don't believe it anymore. And my life has been much more joyful, relaxed, and playful since, and yes, I know that I'm still growing.

When I catch myself fixating over something, giving it too much attention, because it doesn't work the way I want, when I catch myself efforting too much, I stop. When I catch myself pushing hard to do it, be it, dream it, or experience it, I stop.

Now my belief is that it should be effortless. If it is not, I either stop doing it, or if it's something that still has to be dealt with, I take my attention off of it while I focus on anything else that brings me joy and raises my vibration. Soon, the things I was pushing for, became easier. It is the Law of Attraction.

I live by it. My friends know. I often say, "It should be easy. The Universe never meant it to be hard. The easier it gets, the easier it gets."

And the more I practise, the easier it gets, truly.

My decision-making is simpler too (e.g. which one feels easier) and it definitely makes my life more enjoyable.

I wasn't like that before. I used to look for struggle because I was sure it was part of the "recipe" for growth. That being hard made it worthwhile. I believed what I'd been taught.

Pushing hard may be your thing. You may enjoy it, and that's great. It may make you feel special, different, stronger, more expansive. If it works for you, amazing.

But if it doesn't, know that there is an alternative. You can choose the path of least resistance.

And when you're feeling overall happy, joyful, at peace, calm, when a storm comes, you'll be well prepared to face it. Your creativity will blossom. No need to push hard, unless it really brings you joy.

I CAN'T STOP THINKING

Who can?

We are addicted to our thoughts. And we pay them far too much attention.

There are rarely thoughts worth mentioning, or worth engaging with. They are often compulsive, repetitive, and highly judgemental. The first definition of "think" is: to have a particular opinion, belief, or idea about someone or something.

We are *thinking* all the time. What to say next, what we did this morning, what's for lunch, what's on my list, why did he say that?

If you pay attention to your thoughts, you'll notice that they're usually always the same and that they are mostly useless.

Thoughts are vibrations. Their quality is important because when we make a thought active and we keep it active, it impacts the way we feel. Plus, thoughts attract many other thoughts that are similar in nature.

Good thoughts feel *good* when you think of them.
Bad thoughts feel *bad* when you think them.

Therefore, it's worthwhile to pay attention to how you feel.

And if you don't feel good, then it's time to stop thinking those thoughts.

"Well, I know that! But how do I stop thinking that thought?"

Here is what helps me.
I can't stop thinking about something if I am obsessed with it. It's hard. It requires me to push against it, which I don't do anymore. It won't work and will only bring more of the thing I'm pushing against.

Therefore, I'm not trying. Instead, I look for something that feels good and brings me in alignment and focus on it. I can't feel fearful and grateful at the same time.

And sometimes it might not work, as there are thoughts I need to sit with.
Then I make sure I remember that these are only thoughts, beliefs, and judgements.

I bring awareness to them, disassociate and watch them come and go. I don't identify with them anymore.

The second definition of *think* is "to direct one's mind towards someone or something".

Thoughts can be guided. It just takes practice.

I can't stop thinking.

It's okay. Most of us can't - not just yet.
Think better *feeling* thoughts instead.

And *feel* before you act. *Feel* before you talk.

"IN TODAY'S RUSH,
WE ALL THINK TOO
MUCH, SEEK TOO MUCH,
WANT TOO MUCH
– AND FORGET THE JOY
OF JUST BEING."

Eckhart Tolle

IT'S A CHOICE

It's a choice.

And it is mine.

I am the one who *decides*. And I am where I am because of the choices I've made. And I'll be where I'm going to be because of the choices I make now.

It's my choice.

But I might not be aware of it (yet). I might think it's not up to me. After all, surely, I didn't choose this thing that brought me so much pain! How would I?

Yet, I did. I chose what to say, what to do, what to like, where to go, how to address this, what to think, and how to respond all the time.

I choose **all the time**.

But I might not be aware of it (yet).

Without awareness, there is no choice.

Without awareness, I will be doing the same thing over and over again. I would eat the same thing, respond in a similar way, and follow patterns and habits established long ago. I will be in a rut. Of course, it would feel as if it wasn't me who chose that. I would feel as if I didn't have the capacity to make a choice. And it would be true from this perspective.

Because, again, I can only have a choice when I'm conscious, aware.

When I know that the choice is mine to make, I can make it fully present.

I can choose to feel better.
I can choose to feel worse (yes, we sometimes do).
I can choose to focus on joy, happiness, and appreciation.
I can choose frustration, pain, and suffering.

I can choose who I want to be, what I want to experience and what I want to bring into this world.

Then I can choose to give it my full attention.

Or not.

I can choose to do a lot and be happy about it. I can choose to do a lot and be unhappy about it.

My life is truly determined by the choices I make.

I'll do my best to be *aware* of it.

And I'll keep reminding myself, over and over, "I have a choice!"

It's a practice.

You, too, have a choice.

"I AM NOT WHAT
HAPPENED TO ME. I AM
WHAT I CHOOSE TO
BECOME."

Carl Jung

I AM A ROCK

I am a rock.

I am a rock to someone. When they need someone sound to hold on to, someone strong and solid to lean on.

And someone else might be my rock when I need one too.

We are all rocks to someone. And someone is a rock to us, to rest on, to rely on, even if we can't name them yet.

I am a rock to myself as well, as you are to yourself. I can rely on myself, and you can rely on yourself because we all have much greater abilities than we think we have. We all have the innate human capacity to be strong, resilient, solid, tough, sturdy.

I am water.

I am like water to someone. I might be quiet and calm, or fast and turbulent, connected, fluid, and clear.

And someone else is like water to me when I need it.
We are all like water to someone. And someone is like water to us, providing all the emotional support we might need right now.

And as we are all water-like, we have it all in us. We only have to let it flow.

Each and every one of us provides vital support to someone. And each and every one of us has the support of someone. Please always remember it!

Plus, we all have the inner resources available to us to deal with what comes up. If it comes from me, I can handle it. Remember this too.

I am a rock. I am water.

I am both, to you and to me.

And you are too.

We just often forget it.

FOLLOW YOUR DESIRES

Follow your desires.

They are powerful because they come from you. If you have conceived a desire, no matter how momentarily, then you have the capacity to achieve it. It wouldn't have come to you otherwise.

Give it life. Let it stay for a while. Sure, not every desire will make it. But you won't know until you let it hang around, giving it a chance, exploring it, discovering it.

We dismiss most of our desires with impressive speed. The more we live, the better we get at this.

Desire comes, we get excited, we sparkle with joy, we pamper it, and soon, "the reality" hits us.

"Not now; I won't have the time; times are not good; who am I to want this; many others can do it better; it will take too many resources; what's so exciting about it anyways…"

Familiar?

Ah, the good old resistance. Good, because it comes to "protect" us. Old, because we learned this pattern long ago and we forgot to revisit it. It doesn't serve us anymore.

Give your desire a chance. Let your desire evolve and guide you. Allow it to be. You are worthy of it and you conceived it.

Dream it. Focus your attention on everything that could go right with it. Think of it without a doubt. Feel the feeling when it goes right.

Let it spread its wings.

It might not fly high, but you won't know until you set it free.

Follow your desires.

They are powerful because they come from you.

I WILL BRING...

On the last day of the year, billions of people around the world exchange wishes for the coming new year.

We mostly wish it to bring abundance, love, happiness, good health, luck. Beautiful wishes and their energy is all around us.

We say: "Let the new year bring..."

What if, instead of wishing for a new year to bring us what we want, we focus on what we will bring to the new year instead?

I will bring to the new year more kindness, harmony, love, happiness, and gratitude. I'll bring wonderful moments for the people around me. I'll bring peace and harmony to everything I touch. I'll bring adventure and excitement. I will bring the joy.

I'll bring awareness.

We can bring everything we want. It's up to us to decide.

Of course, let the new year bring us too... all that we want. But let us bring it to the new year as well. Because we are magnificent creators and we are in charge.

And how much more powerful we are when we co-create with the universe. We bring, and the universe also brings.

Now it's your turn.

What do you wish to bring to the new year, the new months or the new day? Today?

Write it down. Be it.

And let us remember this.

Life will be as good as we allow it to be.

We are all worthy of well-being. We don't have to do anything to deserve it.

All is well.

Dearest reader,

It has been a true honour to serve you.

I hope the reflections, observations, and insights in this book have been of great support in your own personal journey of expansion, growth, and awakening.

It takes courage to be willing to embrace inner change. It takes courage to reconnect to the truth that is within us.

It requires us to get rid of stories that don't serve us anymore. It requires us to question beliefs and move beyond limitations and concepts created by our mind.

In this process, we take our power back.

Once we begin to wake up, our lives become transformed. We reach out to this quiet place inside, where there is peace and warmth and love. We deepen our appreciation for everything around us - our relationships, ourselves, our planet. We expand our consciousness, and by doing so, we help others too.

I believe that there is a great timing in everything and that this book reaches you at a time when you really need it. And even though you might not be ready to embark on a journey just yet, let it open a door for you that you can choose to cross at any moment.

Have a beautiful day, my dear friend, and remember: you are a powerful creator, and you get to choose the way you want to experience life.

Love,
Didi

Image location

1. Praia da Princesa, Caparica, Portugal
2. Tsavo National Park, Kenya
3. Ol Pejeta Conservancy, Kenya
4. Chyulu Hills, Kenya
5. Kinkara, Costa Rica
6. Lisbon, Portugal
7. Cartagena, Colombia
8. Suguta Sand Dunes, Kenya
9. Cotswolds, UK
10. Finch Hattons, Kenya
11. Silali Crater, Kenya
12. Moreton-in-Marsh, Cotswolds, UK
13. Kinkara, Costa Rica
14. Istron, Crete
15. Nessebar, Bulgaria
16. Lisbon, Portugal
17. Chyulu Hills, Kenya
18. Kinkara, Costa Rica
19. Holland Park, London, UK
20. Cloud Forest, Chyulu Hills, Kenya
21. Notting Hill, London, UK
22. Nairobi, Kenya
23. Es Trenc, Mallorca, Spain
24. Tsavo National Park, Kenya
25. Holland Park, London, UK
26. V&A, London, UK
27. Chicago, IL, USA
28. Cap de Formentor, Mallorca, Spain

29. Praia da Princesa, Caparica, Portugal
30. Beglik Tash, Bulgaria
31. Odeceixe, Portugal
32. Omaya Eco Village, Bulgaria
33. Praia da Princesa, Caparica, Portugal
34. Notting Hill, London, UK
35. Praia do Camilo, Algarve, Portugal
36. New York, NY, USA
37. Virgin Gorda, British Virgin Islands
38. Mahali Mzuri, Kenya
39. Lagos, Algarve, Portugal
40. Finch Hattons, Kenya
41. Holland Park, London, UK
42. Arles, France
43. Carcassonne, France
44. Moreton-in-Marsh, Cotswolds, England
45. Lisbon, Portugal
46. Vratsa, Bulgaria
47. Holland park, London, UK
48. Arles, France
49. Blenheim Palace, UK
50. Ravello, Italy
51. Miami, FL, USA
52. The Rollright Stones, Cotswolds, UK
53. Canillo, Andorra

54. Praia da Princesa, Caparica, Portugal
55. Notting Hill, London, UK
56. LX Factory, Lisbon, Portugal
57. Magado Crater, Kenya
58. Moreton-in-Marsh, Cotswolds, UK
59. Kinkara, Costa Rica
60. Arles, France
61. Nairobi, Kenya
62. Moreton-in-Marsh, Cotswolds, UK
63. Blockley, Cotswolds, UK
64. Holland Park, London, UK
65. Sofia, Bulgaria
66. Lisbon, Portugal
67. El Tarter, Andorra
68. Nazare, Portugal
69. Florence, Italy
70. Kensington, London, UK
71. LX Factory, Lisbon, Portugal
72. Bolsena, Lazio, Italy
73. Blockley, Cotswolds, UK
74. Cabo da Roca, Portugal
75. Kensington, London, UK
76. Cascais, Portugal
77. Kensington, London, UK
78. Ol Pejeta Conservancy, Kenya
79. Praia da Princesa, Caparica, Portugal

80. Hyde Park, London, UK
81. Manuel Antonio National Park, Costa Rica
82. Moreton-in-Marsh, Cotswolds, UK
83. Positano, Italy
84. Vratsa, Bulgaria
85. Pomorie, Bulgaria
86. Nairobi, Kenya
87. Praia da Princesa, Caparica, Portugal
88. Agguire, Costa Rica
89. Nabiyotum Crater, Lake Turkana, Kenya
90. Brook Green, London, UK
91. Lisbon, Portugal
92. Finch Hattons, Kenya
93. Ol Pejeta Conservancy, Kenya
94. Blockley, Cotswolds, England
95. South Island, Lake Turkana, Kenya
96. La Laguna, Tenerife, Spain
97. Melezzole, Umbria, Italy
98. Lagos, Algarve, Portugal
99. Fontelas, Loures, Portugal
100. Necker Island, British Virgin Islands

First published in the UK in 2022 by Xandar Publishing

Text Copyright © Didi Tonev, 2022
Photograph Copyright © Didi Tonev, 2022

Senior Editor: Silja Björk Björnsdóttir
Layout & Design: Bjarney Hinriksdóttir – Baddydesign

ISBN: 978-1-3999-2686-7

Printed and bound in London, United Kingdom.